#DEAR ~~MR~~ ENTREPRENEURSHIP

A Conversation between Ms Entrepreneur and "~~Mr~~ Entrepreneurship"
Letters to "~~Mr~~ Entrepreneurship"

"The Marriage": The challenges, the mistakes, the difficult decisions, the lessons, the failures and the successes

Dr Jabulile Msimango-Galawe (DrJ)

Copyright © 2022

ISBN

9798366605205

Publisher's details:

Author:

Dr Jabulile Msimango-Galawe

Contacts:

+27 11 717 3980

Email:

info@drjbiz.co.za

Table of contents:

Special acknowledgement with a lesson

To my parents who have been my biggest supporters, always "quietly" cheering me on and feeling proud of my progress and achievements. Without the development and exposure they gave my siblings and I, you would not be reading this book. Almost all my life, since primary school, I have been selling something, if it was not sweets, it was popcorn or ice blocks, but I was always selling and that's the exposure I got which rubbed off on me from my parents as they were always selling something or doing some kind of business in one way or the other. My father always had more than one job, he was a teacher/school principal and taxi owner.

In his last years, he retired to start farming. Together with my mom, they were always up to something or selling something. They had a farm, spaza shop, cattle, vegetables, and selling was always involved although a lot of giving away too, as they were very generous people. My father was involved in the taxi industry and constantly selling until his last day. Timewise he was really busy but luckily, he had a wife who could help him and take care of other things. To date, my mom and younger brother continue to run the family business even after my dad's passing.

The lesson: I have 8 siblings (if I count my sister who has passed on) and 5 of us run our own businesses or some kind of side hustle which should show you the power of exposure. What are you exposing your children to? If they are exposed, they are learning consciously or subconsciously therefore what you expose them to, is what you teach them and subsequently what they learn. It will be up to them what they do with what they have learned but your duty as a parent is to expose them to positive things and be intentional about it as it is never by chance or mistake. Kids learn more and more easily from what you do and expose them to rather than what you say, so think about what you are exposing your kids, friends and family to and how this will shape their lives.

Acknowledgements

To Prof Maurice Radebe – who believed in me and agreed to do the foreword by just me telling him my storyline and trusted that I will produce quality good enough for him to put his name on it. What a leader! He also made me uncomfortable postponing the launch date. He said in November 2021 "we are launching, I will hold you accountable to that date, and Jabulile there is no going back, we are launching". That pushed me to put all aside and start writing. Though I launched later than November 2021, I eventually launched sooner than I would have if I did not put a date on it.

To Mr Lesego Tau (Mr Rarebreed, a rare breed indeed) – who kept asking when the manuscript is going to be ready. He made me uncomfortable to keep saying it has not progressed since 2018 when we registered the title. Thank you for making me uncomfortable and you proceeded to making all the designs so that I see them every day and feel even more uncomfortable that there was no content inside the cover design.

To my buddy, Dr Pheladi Mohlala (DrP) – Thank you for the push and the endless writing retreats you tagged along to support me even though your book was not urgent yet. If it was not for your support, it was going to be harder. All the work you did for me for free in helping me push, none is gone unnoticed. Social capital is difficult to put a monetary value on, but is so valuable. I have derived so much value from our friendship (Strong ties indeed).

To my friend, Mr Nceba Galawe (Galax) – Thank you for always being there supporting me and giving me space to chase my dreams. When my first business failed, I had no income and my health was compromised, you took over all my responsibilities (financial and kids wise) and I literally became your dependent until I could get back on my feet. Thank you!

To my little author daughter, Lulama, who made me feel "peer pressure" that she has two books already and my first is still sitting unfinished. She told me she is my role model since I am publishing after her. She could not understand why it is taking so long if she can write hers so quickly. She has two books, one called Summerton – the bizarre planet and another called A Surprise Visit. Check them out and buy them for your kids or gift someone's kids, you won't regret it.

To my siblings and friends who helped me refine the book title, so it talks to the right broad audience and is representative of the content inside.

To my reviewers (Mr Nceba Galawe, Dr Pheladi Mohlala, Ms Brigitta Jordaan and Ms Elona Hlatshwayo) who volunteered their time to read this book, so it makes sense to different audiences and is of good quality. Thank you so much; your support has been amazing.

To all who supported me, I thank you. More so to you, reading the book right now, thank you for purchasing it. I hope you find it valuable.

To DrJ who has always been there to pick self-up when self-grew tired.

Finally, to the God almighty from whom I draw my strength. I was able to author the book and finish it because amid COVID I was blessed with a healthy mind and body.

Dedication

In memory of my late father and sister.

Babe (Dad in Siswati), you and *Make* (Mom in Siswati) exposed us to entrepreneurship but at the time we were not even aware that what you exposed us to was called entrepreneurship. We hated it as when other kids were playing, we had to go sell vegetables and come back home on time to "check in" with taxi drivers. I know you would have been proud and said *"yoooo uyasebenta sesi bese uyananatela utsi Madlela phezulu kandladlane (Translation from Swati to English: you are working my daughter, well done).*

To my late sister, Gugu – I know wherever you are you are proud of me, assuming people who are no longer with us see what is happening on earth. I can hear your voice saying, *yoooo wena Jabu senibhale nemabhuku hhayi niyasicindzetela natsi sekufuna sinyakate phela*

Translated from Swati to English: Surprised – "Jabu you even wrote a book, you put us under pressure, we must also move"

FOREWORD
Prof Maurice Radebe

When Dr Jabulile told me she was authoring this book, I was filled with excitement. I was excited for her but I was also excited for the people who would get to read it, get equipped and be transformed by its content. It is an honour and a pleasure to write the foreword to this book which tackles one of my favourite topics, Entrepreneurship. Every great book has a strong concept which creates a golden thread that runs through every section and chapter of the book. The "Dear Entrepreneurship" concept that DrJ has developed allows the reader to interact with the content in a way that is engaging, entertaining and thought-provoking. She merges her real-life experiences as an entrepreneur with her academic prowess to deliver a product of high quality.

One of the ingredients of success is unrelenting passion and DrJ has demonstrated this trait in her business and at Wits Business School. Her wealth of knowledge has enriched and continues to enrich our students and the many others whom she mentors and coaches. This book is necessary for several reasons. In recent years, the word 'crisis' has become a sort of buzzword, of course, due to the Covid-19 pandemic. There is another crisis which has loomed over our heads for much longer – the unemployment crisis. If we can equip more entrepreneurs with the tools, knowledge, and other resources they need to succeed, we will make a significant dent in the unemployment stats and help raise the standards of living for many.

This book is also important because it will outlive the author. By deciding to put pen to paper, she has cemented her legacy. When you author a book, you immortalise your thoughts and ideas. You speak not just to your generation, but your voice is echoed to the many generations to follow. So many people are loaded with knowledge and experience, but they are going to take all that wealth with them when they leave. As the late Dr Myles Munroe would say, "The richest place in the world is the graveyard."

Reading the manuscript, I could relate to some of her experiences. One of the passages that saddened me is when her business failed, and she had to let her staff go. It's a situation I have encountered in the past when some of my earlier businesses didn't make it. When your business goes under, it can drag your hope and your mental well-being with it. Anxiety can creep in and hopelessness can take root, turning you into a "zombie" as she describes it in the book. One of the stats she quotes is that "90% of startups don't make it past year 3 of operation." When a business "fails", we tend to take it very personally and begin regarding ourselves as failures.

I have never been a fan of the word "Fail" and something I learnt from an elder brother in the Corporate and Faith spheres, Mr Martin Cuscus, the former CEO of the South African Bureau of Standards (SABS), is that the word FAIL is an acronym which stands for "First Attempt In Learning". When things don't go as planned in your business, you must go through a process of evaluation and assessment. What have you learnt? What do you know now that you didn't know before? It would be a loss to pay school fees and then decide to quit school. We should leverage our past experiences and use them as building blocks for future success. I am glad that DrJ didn't let the negative entrepreneurial experiences of her past deter her from venturing back into business. You only lose when you quit.

On my entrepreneurial journey, I have also had to pay school fees quite a few times. I was introduced to business by my late grandfather Philemon Radebe. From as early as seven years of age, I played an active role in the running of his supermarket in Katlehong. He taught me about pricing, stock-taking, building relationships with customers and other facets of a business. Later in life, my wife and I decided to venture into business, and we opened a grocery store. This was a business I was familiar with but there were so many factors we hadn't considered. Firstly, the location wasn't ideal for that kind of business because the parking wasn't sufficient, and it was unable to accommodate the kind of numbers we desired. We had also borrowed money at very unfavourable rates and we battled with the monthly repayments. Add to that, when our neighbour decided to vacate, we rented out the space and opened up a dry-cleaning business, using working capital from the grocery store. Needless to say, everything crumbled and we ended up losing both businesses.

One of the most important topics DrJ covers is that of partnerships. This is another area where I've learnt some hefty lessons. After the grocery store went under, my wife and I started rebuilding our finances and eventually opened a furniture business. It was during a time of growth in the township and people were building and extending their houses, and of course, they needed furniture. The business thrived and we were even able to move into supplying office furniture. Then an opportunity arose to partner with a well-established player in furniture supplies. On paper, it looked good and promised even greater growth for our business.

I was so captivated by the potential growth that I gave them the trust they had not earned, and it ended up costing us the business. Our values were not aligned, and that's a critical aspect. Before you enter into any partnership, spend time ascertaining whether the potential partner shares your values. What ethical and legal boundaries are they not willing to cross? What is their character? Can you rely on them? Another error I made was that I didn't keep my hand on the till and by the time I realised what kind of people they were, it was too late. The money had disappeared. One of the axioms I live by now says, "In God, we trust and everyone else we check."

As a budding entrepreneur, you might hear all these stories and become gripped by fear. In my case, these "failures" eventually led to great success and magnificent rewards. The lessons I learned through these earlier businesses equipped me for future businesses such as Exel Petroleum and others that succeeded. So many people get into a state of fear and they forget that they have great potential and run into a life that is below their true capacity. They forget that they have a God-given assignment and run to mediocrity. Don't let fear make you forget who you are and what you're capable of.

Yes, you will meet with obstacles along the way. None of us is exempt from challenges and struggles. You will make mistakes. You will falter and fall but the only way to reach your dreams and goals is to get up and get going again. There are no medals for quitters. In closing, I would like to congratulate DrJ on this magnificent work. It will surely bless and empower many who have chosen to undertake this journey of entrepreneurship.

Prof Maurice Radebe

Head and Director of Wits Business School

Founder and Chairman of Unleashing Leadership Potential

P A R T

INTRODUCTION

The purpose of this book is to inspire, educate, motivate, get you thinking and hopefully, have you decide and act. I hope after reading this book, you will have learnt a few things and understand the entrepreneurship space better. I share in a fun way with a twist, insights from my entrepreneurial journey of more than 15 years which I hope will assist you to fully appreciate the challenges that come with being an entrepreneur. I talk about the mistakes that I made that you could avoid, the lessons I have learned which you might learn from too, or at least, get you motivated. If you are not an entrepreneur but just an interested party, this book might be useful in giving you a perspective of the fun, freedom, pain, uncertainty and all that comes with marrying MrE so you can make an informed decision as to whether this kind of lifestyle is for you or not.

This book is for everyone but more specifically entrepreneurs and aspiring entrepreneurs. I trust that it will benefit all stakeholders in the entrepreneurship ecosystem whether you are directly or indirectly involved with small business owners, innovators, startups, or entrepreneurs. The stakeholders in the ecosystem that I am referring to are incubators, SMME funding institutions, including non-financial SMME support institutions, and business development or enterprise and supplier development (ESD) providers. Anyone who is a business manager, even if not an entrepreneur, will hopefully learn something from this book, as some lessons or principles will apply in any business context, even though not necessarily entrepreneurship.

THE CONCEPTUALISATION OF THE BOOK

It is important that I explain how the book was conceptualised as it takes an unusual approach of narrating entrepreneurship as a love story. This book is written by an entrepreneur (DrJ who is referred to as Ms Entrepreneur in this book) who had fun, and at the same time, suffered at the hands of "Mr Entrepreneurship". She experienced all that comes with choosing to be an entrepreneur, especially without having fully understood what the journey entails. Nevertheless, that is how entrepreneurs are, they never wait until they fully understand and have all the answers; they go with the flow, or rather, should I say, what they perceive to be the flow. At this moment I can bet that you are wondering why the editors did not pick up the error "Mr Entrepreneurship". Didn't the author intend to say Mr Entrepreneur? No, it is not an error, it is "Mr Entrepreneurship". Read on and you will understand why.

Yes, "Mr Entrepreneurship" Not Mr Entrepreneur.

If you are interested in understanding WHY, then fasten your seatbelt and read on.

One day I was sitting and reflecting on my journey as an entrepreneur and a lot of unanswered questions flooded my thoughts. I attempted to answer them with not much success. Then, as I was wondering why it is so difficult to figure things out and answer all these questions about entrepreneurship, I started wishing that entrepreneurship was a person that I could talk to and ask all these questions, so I granted my wish and did just that.

I thought since I can't talk to him, let me write him letters, maybe one day he will respond; that's how this book was born to write and talk to "Mr Entrepreneurship" himself. As a result of this, I had two options for a subtitle

1. A Conversation between Ms Entrepreneur and "Mr Entrepreneurship"
2. Letters to "Mr Entrepreneurship" from Ms Entrepreneur

Main title:

#Dear "Mr Entrepreneurship" (Catered for the letters part and the hashtag to take the conversation forward with entrepreneurs on social media platforms)

Subtitle:

A Conversation between Ms Entrepreneur and "Mr Entrepreneurship" (Catered for the conversation)

See ME (The Entrepreneur) in a twist with Entrepreneurship the CONCEPT ("Mr Entrepreneurship") personified and narrated as a love story

The relationship between an entrepreneur and entrepreneurship represents a marriage; it is a complex love affair.

Just a warning to those who might be sensitive to the choice of ideology or not subscribe to the ideology of marriage, especially heterogeneous ones. It is an ideology we are most familiar with and for the sake of common understanding, the story is narrated using a man "Mr Entrepreneurship" as a husband and the Entrepreneur as a woman, Ms Entrepreneur.

CHARACTER DEFINITIONS

Entrepreneurs:

Ms Entrepreneur (MsE) is DrJ representing entrepreneurs out there using her entrepreneurial journey, experiences and all the mistakes and lessons learned as a proxy of what entrepreneurs experience and deal with while trying to navigate the stormy waters out there in the VUCA (Volatile, Uncertain, Complex and Ambiguous) world.

Entrepreneurship:

"Mr Entrepreneurship" (MrE) represents the concept of entrepreneurship. The concept takes a human persona to make it less academic but easy to relate to and understand as we journey together and discuss it. We look at what research says about some of the things entrepreneurs experience, and we try to extract all the lessons and operationalise them for practical purposes. Some of the research content will come from DrJ's PhD published in 2017, so if academic jargon excites you then you can read the full text of her thesis titled "Endogenous and exogenous risk factors in the success of South African small and medium enterprises" (Galawe, 2017). If however, academic literature gives you nightmares then leave the thesis, stay here and read on as we're not going to be too academic in this book but rather use layman's terms that non-academics and practising entrepreneurs are comfortable with and easily understand.

Corporates:

Mr Employer (MrEm) represents the corporates or organisations that have staff employed on a full-time or part-time basis and pay them a salary.

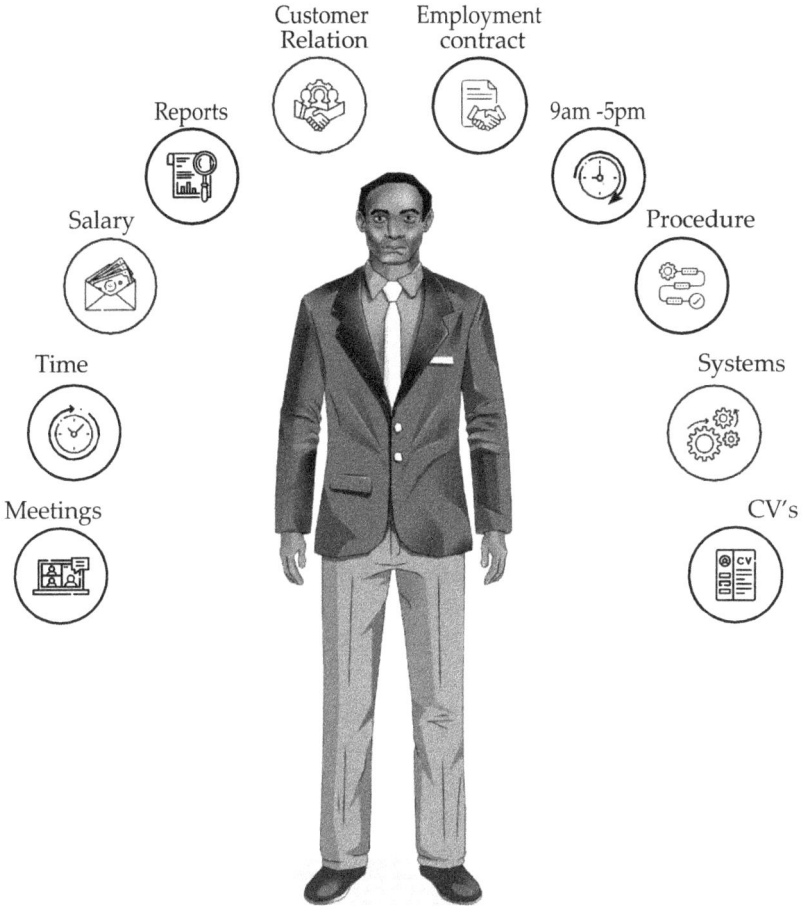

Figure 1: Mr Employer
Source: *Author's own construction*

Thus the Title

#Dear "M̶r̶ Entrepreneurship"
A Conversation between Ms Entrepreneur and "M̶r̶ Entrepreneurship"

BACKGROUND

Let's hear the story of Ms Entrepreneur (MsE) and "Mr Entrepreneurship" (MrE). After years of being an entrepreneur, MsE wished that Entrepreneurship were a person so she could talk to him, ask him questions, vent all her frustrations, and also thank him for making her a better person in the end. The need to talk to MrE grew stronger every day and one day MsE had a light bulb moment. "Why don't I make Entrepreneurship a person so I can talk to him?" She then decided to do just that and as a result, the book titled #Dear "Mr Entrepreneurship" was born.

She decided to call Entrepreneurship "Mr Entrepreneurship", and I am sure you are asking yourself why Mr and not Ms, Mrs, Dr, Prof or It for that matter. The answer is simple, her Entrepreneurship journey felt like a relationship, a romantic relationship with a boyfriend who eventually becomes a husband then finally gets divorced only to remarry later. The remarrying part gets very interesting as the marriage is based on a lot of experience and knowledge thus not done blindly whereas at first it was just a matter of falling in love and going with the flow. Would MsE change anything in the past if she had to start afresh? Nope, definitely not, as the only way to get the ring and be "Mrs Entrepreneurship" and become a real entrepreneur is by doing, failing, and knocking your head against the wall multiple times. Only then do you become an entrepreneur.

One of my colleagues (Dr Mc Edward Murimbika) once said, I quote, "For any other profession you have to study to become, you study medicine you become a medical doctor, you study physiotherapy you become a physiotherapist, you study engineering you become an engineer but entrepreneurship you study entrepreneurship you don't become an entrepreneur however you practice entrepreneurship then you become an entrepreneur". Therefore, you earn the title Ms or should I say Mrs Entrepreneurship by doing.

Because of the fluid nature of Mrs Entrepreneur's marital status, we will use Ms Entrepreneur throughout this book irrespective of whether the discussion refers to when she was married, divorced or remarried to Mr Entrepreneurship at the time. Only by doing, you are made an entrepreneur and not by talking or reading, but by doing. It is an action-orientated concept, you do to become. Ripsas (1998) once said entrepreneurs are not defined by what they have but by what they do. It's a doing phenomenon, action-oriented, it's a verb even in its noun form by definition.

MsE's experience is that once you have come into contact with MrE, it is hard to have a relationship with other Misters because he changes your life so much that you will never be the same again. Resisting him just becomes close to impossible, irrespective of how much you feel he abused you and left you unconscious, because when you regain your consciousness, you are most likely to go back and mend what was broken and start over again. Some say, "once an entrepreneur always an entrepreneur", you might not necessarily go back to start a new business if you are too scared because of scars and bruises you haven't fully recovered from but you are prone to be entrepreneurial whenever you get an opportunity to do so. It's like marriage, once you have been married, you can never erase the experience and the learnings, it changes your perspective for good, as the lens you look at life through will never be the same. Unfortunately, the change is out of your control, the only thing that is within your control is how you allow those scars and bruises to shape you, whether they make you better or worse, it's your choice.

This book is about the relationship MsE had with MrE and the journey they agreed to take together for a long time to come. It includes all the challenges MsE faced, the mistakes she made and lessons learned with some integration of her PhD research learnings and insights. This book will make you cry, smile, gasp, laugh, sigh and smile again. You will be encouraged and discouraged to become an entrepreneur which is exactly what the journey of entrepreneurship feels like, you go through all the emotions like four seasons in one day, much like Cape town's (City in South Africa) weather.

8

Context of the love story

MsE started dating MrE privately in 2004. She registered her first business in 2003 but nothing happened except registration until 2004. In 2008 the marriage started having problems and despite attempts to make it work, in 2011 they decided to call it quits and file for divorce. However, in 2015 they started dating again privately until in 2016 when they made it official and public again but this time the marriage contract clearly stipulated that MsE would want to have a relationship with both MrE and MrEm. To date, MsE continues to be in a relationship with both but that comes with its own advantages and disadvantages.

Now let us buckle up and journey together, one letter at a time as we have the conversation with MrE. Before we get on to the conversation, let us answer the question, what is and what is not entrepreneurship or an entrepreneur for that matter, so we are all on the same page?

ENTREPRENEURSHIP AND ENTREPRENEURS

Academic definitions and origin

If academic reading irritates the heaven out of you, I permit you to skip this section. Hold on, are you skipping it? This was meant to have the reverse psychology effect, hoping you will read and get a taste of academic writing if you have not been exposed to it. However, don't let it put you off or make you put the book down rather read it last. Here is a challenge for you, read it so you get an understanding of what entrepreneurship is from a research perspective than what is generally perceived to be with no basis. I assume we all know the myths about who qualifies to be called an entrepreneur and who does not so let's read and separate the myths from the "truth".

Now that we have a deal that you will read the academic section, buckle up and let's go to the academic world, trust me – it is just for this section to make sure we conceptualise entrepreneurship using appropriate theoretical foundations before we start talking about it loosely or referring to it while we all understand it differently.

.

THE DEFINITIONS AND CONCEPTUALISATION

There are many definitions of 'entrepreneurs' and 'entrepreneurship' in literature, as many as they are out there in our day-to-day vocabulary. Currently, there is no single universal definition of entrepreneurship, although there are some elements of similarities in concepts developed so far and this is what makes the conceptualisation of entrepreneurship studies complicated. Some of the main authors who have contributed significantly towards deepening today's understanding of entrepreneurship theory, include Kirzner, Schumpeter, Busenitz and Barney and many more[1]. However, they have not addressed the issue of multiple definitions as they are all from different disciplines so they each define entrepreneurship based on their background. For example, those who are in psychology define entrepreneurs using behavioural science theories while those who are economists define it according to economic theories.

First, the Global Entrepreneurship Monitor, popularly known as GEM, defines entrepreneurship as "any attempt at new business or new venture creation, such as self-employment, a new business organization or the expansion of an existing business, by an individual, a team of individuals, or an established business"[2]. This is one of the simplest and basic definitions you will likely ever find in academic literature. Interestingly GEM makes an example of self-employment as a form of entrepreneurship. What is your thought, do you think self-employment is entrepreneurship? Some argue that self-employed individuals are not "real" entrepreneurs, you need to have more than yourself to be called an entrepreneur.

(Busenitz & Barney, 1997; Kirzner, 1978; 1999; Schumpeter, 1934; Shane & Venkataraman, 2000)[1]
(Reynolds, Hay, & Camp, 1999)[2]

Let's look at more definitions and qualities of entrepreneurs, maybe at the end of this book we will be able to share our views with a certain level of confidence about whether self-employed individuals are entrepreneurs or not, are they practising entrepreneurship or are they technically, theoretically and practically just employees?

Entrepreneurs and entrepreneurship - Long (1983) describes how the two concepts are defined and differentiated. He defines entrepreneurship as a process and the entrepreneur in terms of competencies, capacities, and skills, as cited by Chen, Greene, and Crick (1998). The concept of entrepreneurship is viewed as a situation that describes the general structural functioning of the economy and society, while the entrepreneur is described as the person (agent) involved in the activity. Ripsas (1998) also agrees that an entrepreneur is defined by the work she does and not by what she owns. I like this definition as it takes us to what I mentioned earlier about my colleague who said entrepreneurs don't become entrepreneurs by studying or qualifications but by what they do or practice. Ripsas (1998) adds further to say it is also not by what they own but what they do. You can have billions of Rands/Dollars and still not be an entrepreneur, it's what you do and not what you own that makes you one. You can have zero or negative balance in your bank account but still qualify to be called an entrepreneur, if we follow the definition that says, it is by doing and not by owning that makes you an entrepreneur.

Another school of thought that takes a totally different view, is the Leadership school of thought. One scholar seems to dispute that entrepreneurship is a concept that is worth special attention. He believes entrepreneurship falls within the leadership field. He claims entrepreneurship is just leadership in a narrow, specific context[3]. I disagree with this view; entrepreneurship definitely has leadership as one of the key characteristics of the entrepreneur, but that cannot reduce the whole complex phenomena to just one characteristic within it.

(Vecchio, 2003)[3]

Just pause and think about the two, leadership and entrepreneurship, what is your take, do you think Vecchio's paradigm fits this complex concept? I think entrepreneurship definitely needs to be treated as a separate construct from general leadership theories because it is a context and task-specific construct, not to say that leadership is not, but entrepreneurship is more complex and has more dimensions than just leadership. This for me, shows the interdisciplinary nature of entrepreneurship as a concept[4] as well.

Table 1: Summarises some of the definitional developments that have taken place since the conversation on entrepreneurship started. Different scholars conceptualise entrepreneurship differently, and the conceptualisation has evolved. I am more interested in the key themes that emerge from these conceptualisations of the theory of entrepreneurship or entrepreneurs and their basic definitions. I am of the view that the key themes can direct us to the critical elements that make entrepreneurs and entrepreneurship definitions.

Table 1: Key themes on the conceptualisation of entrepreneurship (the process) and entrepreneur (the agent)

Definitions	Authors	Key themes
Entrepreneurs are self-employed individuals who adjust themselves to risk where the return is uncertain.	(Palich & Bagby, 1995)	Risk Uncertainty
Entrepreneurs are individuals who pursue an opportunity regardless of the resources they control.	(Timmons, 1994)	Proactive Initiation
Entrepreneurs are confident individuals who act upon their own judgement in the face of uncertainty attached exploitation of opportunities.	(Knight, 1921)	Uncertainty Opportunity Confident Judgement

(Baum, Locke, & Smith, 2001)[4]

Entrepreneurs are innovators who carry out new unique combinations or integrate resources by introducing new products or processes to generate profit.	(Schumpeter, 2000)	Innovation Profit
The entrepreneur is someone who facilitates adjustment to change by spotting opportunities for profitable arbitrage.	(Kirzner, 1999)	Opportunity Profit
Entrepreneurship is the ability to detect opportunities in the environment in which we are living, produce dreams from those intuitions, converting these dreams into projects, carrying out these projects into application, and facilitating the living of people.	(Bozkurt, 2000)	Opportunity Innovation Intuition
Entrepreneurs are those who have either founded a firm within the last two years or plan to launch within the next five years.	(Busenitz & Barney, 1997)	Initiation
Entrepreneurs are organisational actors who create rents through innovation. Rents are conceptualised as earnings above average relative to others in the industry and innovation as an act of carrying out new combinations to create value.	(Malone, 1991)	Innovation Profit
Entrepreneurs are individuals who are driven jointly by motivation and outcome. They are characterised with three discrete categories which are lifestyle, small profitable and high growth ventures.	(Ronstadt, 1984)	Profit Motivation Outcome Growth
The entrepreneur is the one who undertakes a venture, organises it, raises capital to finance it, and assumes all or a major portion of the risk.	(Burch, 1986)	Initiation Risk
Entrepreneurship is bringing new goods and services not available in the enterprise, organisation of shape, markets, processes and raw materials, opportunity discovery and evaluation of activities.	(Shane & Venkataraman, 2000)	Opportunity Innovation
An entrepreneur is a person who is developing strategies in line with his/her own entrepreneurship understanding, so he/she is the person who has made the pioneering of change.	(Ozkara et al., 2006)	Initiation

Source: *Galawe (2017)*

There is strong evidence presented from the definitions in Table 1, that risk and uncertainty are what the entrepreneurial environment is made of, and this is the kind of environment in which entrepreneurs must operate. Every definition has either a direct or an inferred risk conceptualisation, thus entrepreneurs need to be comfortable dealing with risk. If I were to try to summarise the common themes that stand out from the tabulated definitions, I will include risk, uncertainty, innovation, profit, initiation, motivation, confidence, and opportunity, as these feature in most of the definitions.

Therefore, this book's definition and understanding encompass these key themes which are core and capture the key roles and tasks that entrepreneurs perform. From these key features, a definition for this book can be adopted so we all read the book from the same reference point of what entrepreneurship is. Below we define entrepreneurs, and the process they embark on which is called entrepreneurship. The fact that the term 'entrepreneur' does not have one definition can be taken as a reflection of how diverse and complex entrepreneurs and their ventures can be.

An entrepreneur is an individual who can endogenously (internally) create and exogenously (externally) identify or discover opportunities in an environment where everyone else sees chaos and high risk and convert or repackage the chaos and risks into innovation that can cater for people's needs (market gap), make a profit, and create a successful enterprise[5]. Entrepreneurship then becomes the process that the entrepreneurs embark on to achieve desirable entrepreneurial outcomes (success).

I know success is a very subjective word and difficult to objectively define but we can comfortably work with it as subjective as it is. Any desirable outcome that an entrepreneur sets for him or herself and achieves it, we will view as success.

(Schumpeter, 2000; Knight, 1921)[5]

The next question can be, what is a desirable outcome? As it is subjective too, we will take the interpretivist view and be comfortable with the subjective nature of the definitions and agree that there are many definitions and many truths because of the subjective nature of success and desirable outcome.

It is important to note that research has advanced and is moving away from the paradigm of one type of entrepreneurship and more have been introduced to define entrepreneurs taking into consideration their context, focus areas and objectives. In the new millennium, the entrepreneurship domain has expanded to encompass various forms of entrepreneurship, including, but not limited to international new ventures or born globals[6], entrepreneur-state nexus[7], intrapreneurship, social entrepreneurship and nascent, novice and expert entrepreneurship[8]. Such concepts are gaining ground and the emphasis is on the process from ideation to product creation and acquisition of first customers at a global level. The rise and fall of nations are directly related to the rise and fall of entrepreneurship[9]. But do we even know the origins of these concepts; let us look at the history and where it all started.

(Bouncken, Muench, & Kraus, 2015)[6] (Ács & Naudé, 2013)[7]
(Hopp, 2015; Lans, Seuneke, & Klerkx, 2013)[8] (Heredero, 1979)[9]

THE ORIGINS OF ENTREPRENEURSHIP

To detect a conceptual foundation of the entrepreneurial concept, we resort to the origins of the word "entrepreneur". The term "entrepreneur" originated in French economics by the physiocrats as early as the 17th and 18th centuries, meaning someone who "undertakes" a significant project or activity[10], whereas Filion (2008) emphasises that the term "entrepreneur" first appeared in the literature in 1253 when it was used in different forms, but it appears to have taken on its present, definitive spelling in 1433. The word "entrepreneur" also has a connotation of the 13th century French verb 'entreprendre', meaning "to do something" or "to undertake"[11].

Van Praag's (1999) systematic timeline approach which is based on Kurian and Kushwaha's (2015) collage (see Figure 2), also includes Braunerhjelm's (2010), Toma, Grigore and Marinescu's (2014) definitions and characteristics of entrepreneurship to review classic contributions to the theory of entrepreneurship which outline the fundamental concepts that shaped the definition since its origins from Richard Cantillon, Jean-Baptiste Say, Alfred Marshall, Joseph Schumpeter, Frank Knight, and Israel Kirzner (Mokgwatsane, 2019, p.19).

(Dees, 2017)[10] (Filion, 2008)[11]

How did the word entrepreneur originate?

The researcher maps the origin and the root of the word "entrepreneur" as defined since the 13th century. The research indicates that the word 'entrepreneur' had many different definitions across the centuries. We present to you a short timeline on its origin and history

13th Century
The word entrepreneur comes from the 13th century French verb 'entreprendre', meaning "to do something" or "to undertake".

16th Century
The noun entrepreneur had emerged to refer to someone who undertakes a business venture.

Baptiste Say (1767 - 1832)
Economist Jean Baptiste Say, refer entrepreneurs as individuals who create value in an economy by moving resources out of areas of low productivity into areas of higher productivity and greater yield. He also says that entrepreneurs and managers have different but complementing characteristics.

Richard Cantillon (1680? - 1734)
The first academic usage of the term by economist Richard Cantillon. He defined an entrepreneur as someone who undertakes a business venture with no guarantee of profits, as a self-employed with uncertainty. "The entrepreneurial class accomplishes its task by engaging in pure arbitrage".

Alfred Marshall (Late 1800s): Neo-classical economist Alfred Marshall emphasizes the importance of entrepreneurship by tying the resource component (from Baptise Say) and management component (from Stuart Mill) together. Marshall claims that entrepreneur are drivers and coordinators of four primary factors necessary for production: land, labor, capital and organization and they undertake all the risks that are associated with the latter.

Joseph Schumpeter (1883 - 1950 - Early 20th century: Schumpeterian view identifies entrepreneurs as innovators and agents of change, emphasis being that an entrepreneur is willing and able to convert a new idea or invention into a successful innovation. In his words, "the function of entrepreneurs is to reform or revolutionize the pattern of production."

Israel Kirzner (1973 - 1997) - Late 20th century
According to Kirzner, entrepreneurs are persons in the economy who are alert to discover and exploit profit opportunities, his emphasis is that entrepreneurial activity moves the market towards equilibrium as entrepreneurs discover profitable arbitrage possibilities.

Frank Knight (1885 - 1972 - Late 20th century: Knightian entrepreneurship contributed to a thorough analysis of the motivations and characteristics needed to become a successful entrepreneur, referred an entrepreneur as uncertainty-bearer and judgmental decision maker.

Figure 2: Timeline and origin of entrepreneurship
Source: *Kurian & Kushwaha (2015) as cited in Mokgwatsane (2019, p.20)*

The term came to be used to identify venturesome individuals who stimulated economic progress by identifying, finding and profitably introducing new and/or better products, services and processes, also as change agents (reformers and revolutionaries), risk-takers, risk bearers, uncertainty undertakers, innovators, opportunity-driven, resourceful, value creators, capitalists, decision-makers and organisers; but when people create a new venture or company, they have entered the entrepreneurship paradigm. Analysis of the development of the term 'entrepreneurship' reveals that an entrepreneur is a multi-functional personality discharging different roles varying in relation to time, place, region and country[12]. Therefore, I recognise that there is a broader meaning to the entrepreneurial concept, which also fulfils Kuratko's equation, which says entrepreneurs cause entrepreneurship[13]. There is no entrepreneurship without entrepreneurs and there are no entrepreneurs without the doing /the action and enacting entrepreneurship.

Let's understand the difference between the people below:

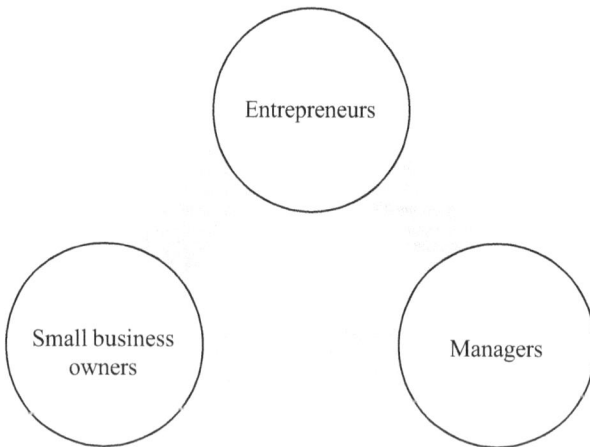

Source: *Author's own construction*

(Heredero, 1979)[12]   (Kuratko, 2007)[13]

Table 2: Differentiation between entrepreneurs, small business owners, managers and self-employed.

Description	Types of entrepreneurs
Entrepreneurs	**Corporate entrepreneurs** – innovation within the company.
	Technopreneurs – identifies technological enhancements and develop these for profit.
	Social entrepreneurs – these are change agents working within the public area.
	Entrepreneurs – innovative, high growth and profitability.
Small business owners	Survivalist
	Opportunity and innovation
	Self-employed
	High growth vs. replication of an existing business
	Necessity vs. opportunity
	Local vs. systemic
Managers	**Traditional management** Is practical and manages existing resources
	Does not look for new opportunities
	Is not creative or risk-taking.
	Small businesses Don't have many products
	Are not innovative
	Don't grow the business.

Source: *Venter et al. (2015)*

Now that we have adopted a common definition and understanding of entrepreneurship, we can now start with our conversation with MrE.

B

LETTERS AND CONVERSATIONS WITH "MR ENTREPRENEURSHIP"

I started by introducing the concept of "Mr Entrepreneurship" and Ms Entrepreneur and how the idea came about, then the conversation begins mainly by highlighting all the ups and downs and the fun that MrE brought into MsE's life. I try to draw key insights from the conversation that might add value to your journey, and I conclude by summarising each chapter or letter and providing tips on a few things I have learned. Lastly, I share the biography of MsE to give you a glimpse of where she comes from.

Come journey with me as we have the conversation with MrE as he has been too busy to respond to the letters written to him. Let's have the conversation and ask "him" the questions I asked in the letters I wrote to him for years which he has not responded to so far.

LETTER

INTRODUCTION OF LETTERS TO "MR ENTREPRENEURSHIP"

Dear "Mr Entrepreneurship"

I have been meaning to write to you for a while now and have finally managed to put pen on paper. I have a lot that I want to say to you, not to mention the questions and the frustrations that I have been bottling up for years. I want to offload and get this off my chest. Taking into consideration your busy schedule, I decided to write you several short letters, one entrepreneurial letter at a time or should I say one love letter at a time. This is an introductory letter, alerting you of the letters to come. I cannot quantify at the moment how many are to come but I have a lot to chat to you about, so expect lots. As I said, let us take it slowly, one letter at a time for many months to come.

Let me introduce myself again, my name is Ms Entrepreneur, popularly known as MsE. I started hearing about you and noticing your work early in 2002. The things that people said about you were startling. Everybody spoke highly of you, the government, the media, business women, business organisations and many more in the community.

I was enticed and developed even more interest to know you better so I started paying more attention to what was said. In 2003, I started falling for you, thus the opening of my first small business. I never thought for once in my life that I would fall for a guy like you. You were just not my type. You were not meeting the criterion of what I had imagined for my dream man. I never even knew that there was a man like you, nevertheless, the journey began, it looked greener on the other side.

You promised me flexibility, that I would be my own boss, lots of money, fame, independence, control, wealth, respect, and quality of life, to name a few. You never said anything about sleepless nights, being broke, family conflicts, banning, rejection, bankruptcy, loss of assets, house, car, savings, investments, not to mention friends, and social status in the community. So full of naivety, I fell in love, and embarked on the journey with you. As I look back now, my expectations were unrealistic, I saw a perfect man with no flaws, at least pretended not to see your flaws so I was bound to get disappointed with such unrealistic expectations. My heart was guaranteed to be broken when the expectations I created for myself were not realised. I was blind to all the negatives, what people refer to as red flags.

It all looked good theoretically and on paper, maybe too good to be true. A lived 'happily ever after' kind of scenario, a perfect life forever to be 'lifestyle goals'. Then the journey began, it was exciting in the beginning, everyone in government and SME support institutions promised to support me in order to build this relationship I had just started with you. It all sounded like a quick way to get to the top. It was more appealing than where I was. Where I was, wasn't too bad either: I had a salary every month, a pension fund, life cover, medical aid, car allowance and my working hours were well defined and known. These were among the many benefits that came with being with MrEm.

However, it was not enough, your value proposition sounded more like, what I had been looking for all my life. I was convinced that this was GOD showing me my Canaan and I was ready to go to the land of milk and honey. It was like a honeymoon there, whilst where I was felt like an old boring marriage with boring routines, nothing challenging and exciting anymore. I hoped at the time that it was not what they normally call it (grass looking greener on the other side).

Since I promised that this would be a brief introductory letter, let me honour my word and leave it here for now. The letters to come are going to be short and divided into themes and each letter will unpack the journey, interrogation, challenges and lessons derived from each of them. Thanking you in advance for taking the time to read and hopefully respond to my letters and making the time to come have the conversation with me, after all, I am your woman, you need to make time for your woman.

Yours in Love

MsE

LETTER

2

FALLING IN LOVE WITH SOMEONE
I DID NOT KNOW

Dear MrE

Is it a bad idea to fall in love with someone you don't know; if you know them, would that guaranteed success of the relationship? That is my question, MrE, because entrepreneurs fall in love with you and get into a marriage without knowing much about you, they use their intuition and go with the flow. Is entrepreneurship different from a romantic relationship or are there similarities we can learn from MrE?

MrE, I fell in love with you very early on in my life journey, I was still young, energetic and a graduate fresh from varsity. I was married to MrEm who looked after me very well, but you came along and started enticing and promising me all sorts of things. You were so bold to tell me that you can give me a better life than what MrEm, who was my lover at the time, was giving me. I hate to admit that you were such a charmer, and you won my heart over. Honestly, I had already fallen; so, anything you said was just making me smile, it was tempting.

I can't believe I am even timid as I write you this letter, reliving those days when love was pink, and I had just fallen in love with you. But as tempting as it was, I was scared to leave my then lover for you. I was attracted to the life you were promising me, but I kept asking myself:

What if it did not work?

What if you couldn't give me what MrEm was giving me? What if it all came tumbling down?

How was I going to tell my parents that I left a good husband for you if things didn't work out?

What would my friends say if it all ended in divorce after they warned me not to leave MrEm?

What about my social status?

The battle between the mind and heart was real, it was war. My heart had already fallen and made the decision to date you, but my mind was not in agreement. All the analyses told me I was fine and comfortable with MrEm so I must just stay. They say "if it is not broken don't fix it" but as much as it was not broken, I felt a bit of fixing was going to make a significant difference. My heart ended up winning, they say "matters of the heart are difficult to explain". The logic was not logical at the time, but I followed my heart anyway.

These were all the questions that kept coming up every time the thought of leaving MrEm for you came up. Was I wrong in choosing you, MrE, without knowing much about you?

Yours In Love

MsE

While we wait for MrE to respond to my letter, let's share some thoughts on MsE's behaviour and decisions. If you critically analyse the questions MsE kept asking herself, you will notice they all have a negative connotation. They are all about the possibility of failure. No question said "what if it works? What if MrE is better than MrEm?

They were all disabling questions meant to keep me stuck. Truth is, we all ask ourselves these kinds of questions and there is nothing wrong with asking the negative questions but what disables us is when we don't answer them and don't go further and ask the positive questions too so we can move to a decision-making phase and action what we wanted to action in the first place but understanding both perspectives.

Lessons:

1. Answer all the negative questions and use them to calculate the risk, and plan, accordingly, put different scenarios on the table, and how you will handle each. Don't let them stop you.
2. Be comfortable with the unknown, you won't be able to answer all questions, so learn to be ok with deciding and actioning it without all the answers. You will never have all the answers and if you want to be in a relationship with MrE you need to be comfortable with an uncertain future. Nothing is guaranteed, do your best to understand what you are getting yourself into; nonetheless, you will never be 100% guaranteed a positive outcome.
3. Force yourself to ask the positive questions, imagine the success you envisage then plan for it, do the research, and have an idea of what you need to get there and how long it will take you to get there. All these will be estimates which will become wrong as soon as you get going but you need the wrong estimates to start aiming for something and having a plan. Don't start with zero goals and no action plans, otherwise, your failure will be more costly. They say fail fast and fail cheap, and that comes with having a plan and keeping that plan with as little fat as practically possible or opt for the lean startup route if you can't afford to lose millions and extended time.

4. Is it a bad idea to fall in love with someone you don't know? If you know them, would that guarantee success? It is not as if you will ever know everything but ensure that you know enough to take you to the next phase. Do not go into the relationship with no foundation, have some knowledge on what you are getting into. Don't go in it blank, you will burn your fingers harder than you will if you have some knowledge. Nothing can be guaranteed, so the risk is something you need to be willing to take and a loss you must be open to.

"Don't get into the soccer field if you are not prepared to get an injury. Don't play the netball game if you are not prepared to accept a loss. Don't play in the game of love if your heart is not prepared to be broken. Don't go into entrepreneurship if you are not prepared to fail" DrJ.

5. Is entrepreneurship different from a romantic relationship or are there similarities we can learn from? There are a lot of similarities, first is that nothing is guaranteed, it is about risk-taking, and how much you are prepared to burn your fingers in your quest for a successful business or relationship. Couple your knowledge with intuition, follow the plan and your gut and they will take you there or close to where you want to get to. Say I do, marry MrE, and get on with it; get ready to learn and burn your fingers while having fun doing it.

"The only time you will know if it worked is when it works and the only time you will know that it won't work is when it has not worked" DrJ.

You can only answer most of the 'what if' questions by doing and not by theory. It is a trial and error approach, the sooner you start trying, the sooner you can fail and the sooner you can learn and know if this kind of relationship is for you.

Mistakes:

What I never did before starting to date MrE was to answer all the negative questions I was asking myself. All I needed to do was to answer them. I never did and that kept me anxious and in doubt. What I know today which I did not know then, was that I was supposed to answer all those negative questions that kept lingering. Would I have had the answers then; yes, but not to all the questions. I had to force my mind to go beyond the questions to answers. If I did answer, would the answers have been accurate? No. What I know today is that I was supposed to answer the questions, whether correctly or incorrectly. I was supposed to have answered them because it was going to force me to think through certain things I did not think about or was afraid to think about, it was going to force me to think of plan B while putting together Plan A.

Are you in the same position today, trying to decide which husband is good for you, MrEm or MrE? Have you fallen in love already with MrE, but you have a lot of questions? My advice is to answer the 'what if' questions so you are forced to think of a lot of possibilities and different plans based on possible outcomes. Just answer the damn questions and decide. The answer I have today as I think in retrospect is that even if those questions were to have negative responses; it was still going to be useful answers for my next steps.

No one knows how any marriage will turn out nonetheless, you do your best and answer the questions you can answer and decide if you want in or not. You go in knowing the risks, seeing the red flags because no human being will show up with no risks or red flags. The decision should be about what you are prepared to deal with, what red flags you feel you are willing to live with, which calculated risks make sense to you and you are open to losing? Those are the difficult decisions we make every day, if you are not willing to answer the 'what ifs' and decide what negatives you are prepared to go with, despite knowing them, then you become the most indecisive person on planet earth, you don't progress or grow, and you stay in one spot forever.

Is the squeeze going to be worth the juice at the end? We all don't know the future and the only way to know is to get into the future, and learn from the past, then you will have better answers, you will connect the dots backwards and use the learning for a better future. What is my point? the answers to the questions should not stop you from making the decision but should help you calculate your risk and then decide. Deciding does not mean marrying MrE but it means deciding on whom to marry, there is no guaranteed marriage anyway get into it and you will find out if MrE or MrEm is the ideal guy for you. Just calculate your risk then you know if it goes south what you stand to lose and decide if you are prepared to lose that much.

Do your homework and get in. My mistake was getting married to MrE without doing my homework. But you may ask "so if you did your homework would your first business have survived?" I don't know, but I would have increased the likelihood of it surviving, because I would have had fewer blind spots and understood a bit more of what, why and how to handle things. What I am saying is do your homework, although it does not guarantee you success, it increases the likelihood of positive outcomes. This prepares you to handle the failure or divorce better because you go in knowing you are not immune to failure so if it does fail or end in divorce you won't have regrets because you would have given it your best.

Even though I did not do my homework, the feeling was strong, and I wanted to accept MrE's proposal, but what my heart said was contrary to what my brain was saying. So, to play it safe I started with small steps, I started dating MrE while I was married to MrEm. I registered my first business in 2003 to test the waters and see if marriage with MrE would work or not. The more time I invested in this new secret lover or life, the deeper I went into it. The harder I fell for MrE, the shallower and more uninteresting my relationship with MrEm became. At the time, MrE was like a side-dude and MrEm was the known, full time, till death do us part lover.

Before you commit forever, get to know someone a little, spend time with them and see what they like and what they don't like. See what irritates or triggers them and decide whether you want in or out. Date, get engaged, break up the engagement, marry, divorce, and remarry (this is the process that gets repeated in the entrepreneurship journey, and I am not naïve to the fact that based on different religious beliefs, you might have a different stance when it comes to marriage in real life). The longer you are in, the more difficult it becomes to get out. You get out with scars, lessons, and a new perspective on life as a whole. You learn more about yourself as well in the process. Don't just fall in love; fall, stand up then make an informed decision. A thinking-based decision rather than an emotionally based decision is better. Don't only base your decision on how much your current lover irritates you, think also if you like the lifestyle of real entrepreneurs. I still emphasise you will never know everything, but know enough to get you moving, you will learn more on the way. Research is key, don't take it for granted.

The real-life of an entrepreneur or a married woman, do you know it, do you like it? Not only the good things that are always portrayed in pictures. I am asking about the real life behind the scenes where there are no cameras to pose for or to record and post on social media. You have to like the life in its entirety, otherwise you will be unhappy. It is a long journey; you don't want to just fall in love as emotions come and go, there must be something left when the feeling evades you. As I said earlier, you will never know 100%, but balance what you know with what you feel (intuition and butterflies); don't go on feelings only, otherwise you will crash. Watch out and be sober about it.

Figure 3: The perceived image of an entrepreneur
Source: *Adobe*

When I started dating MrE, I was like a side chick who believed, irrespective of what the husband does to the current wife, he will never do it to me because he loves me and the wife just does not know how to make MrE happy, I was convinced I would make him happy because I knew how and in return, would live happily ever after. Little did I know it had nothing to do with the wife but had everything to do with MrE, the denominator was him. I was naïve, ignorant, over-optimistic, unrealistic, and biased, to list but a few. That's generally how side chicks perceive a situation when dating a married man and they never bother to dig more and understand why the husband is treating the wife the way he is. They just assume they won't experience that. I never thought I would ever experience what I saw other entrepreneurs experiencing. All I saw was a 'happily ever after' and lots and lots of money, but this made me miss the opportunity to do things better and increase my chances of succeeding.

Dear MrE

What I learned is that you are not who most think you are; and this goes both ways (bad and good). The only way to know who you are is to get closer to you, be with you and commit to doing this marriage wholeheartedly. Knowing you from a distance can be misleading and when a person gets too close to you the picture changes. The impact of everything that happens with you is huge, not sure whether it is because of the proximity or because of who you are and your intention to lure people in and then show them your true colours once they are in. You are like a boyfriend who makes you feel like a queen before marriage and once married, everything changes for the worst and you make it up with expensive gifts now and then so one does not leave. You keep making promises, saying "If you do this and that my wife, I promise you things will get better" but because things take too long to get better, most divorce you after a few months or years. I did the same too, I divorced you in 2011 because it was just too much to handle, especially when our relationship started affecting my health and I was forever broke. I found myself in your arms again in 2015 after all the hardships. What is it with you that makes me keep coming back to you?

MrE, but after all these years being with you as a boyfriend, a side dude, a full-time husband, a part-time husband I still don't understand and know you well. My question is who are you? What kind of a person entices someone to get out of a relationship that is working well, that's what I thought and wished to ask you but never had the chance to do so. We were fine with MrEm, at least that is what I thought until you came along, and everything started becoming boring, became routine, there was no challenge and no excitement anymore. But I tolerated it as I was still not sure about this new life whether I want to keep both MrEm and MrE, so I continued with my double life and cheated on MrEm.

Yours in Love
MsE

While we wait for MrE to respond, let me share with you what was happening during this time when I was trying to keep two lovers. I assigned a lot of responsibilities to other people to take care of my house and keep it clean and in order, as I could not give it my full attention since MrEm still expected me to give 100%. But I realised I was doing myself a disfavour and not necessarily MrEm or you. I became more and more dissatisfied, I was not content anymore, my peace was gone, I was troubled. After 3 years of having two lovers, I had to choose, as no one was given 100% attention, and no one was happy in that arrangement. Both lovers wanted 100% commitment, no one wanted to be a side dude or the secret lover, maybe because I gave both the impression that they were my only lover thus the expectation.

Was the unhappiness caused by having two lovers or was it the belief that I needed to have one, would our relationship have worked while keeping MrEm but just making it all official than a secret. The evidence at the time suggested otherwise, as the people who were assigned to take care of MrE while I was busy taking care of MrEm failed to deliver as mandated.

Finally, one blessed day in 2006 I said "I do" to MrE, my boyfriend of 3 years since we had been dating since 2003. I finally left MrEm, and I was excited to start a new life and leave the life that had become strenuous with all the secrets and divided attention.

The question I never asked before getting involved with MrE is, who is he? Why has he become so popular, who knows him better, why is he trying to charm me? To date he is still one man I can't figure out and understand. The picture below shows how confusing it can be to try to figure out what kind of a being MrE is. What picture of him do you have in your imagination, is it close to what is illustrated below?

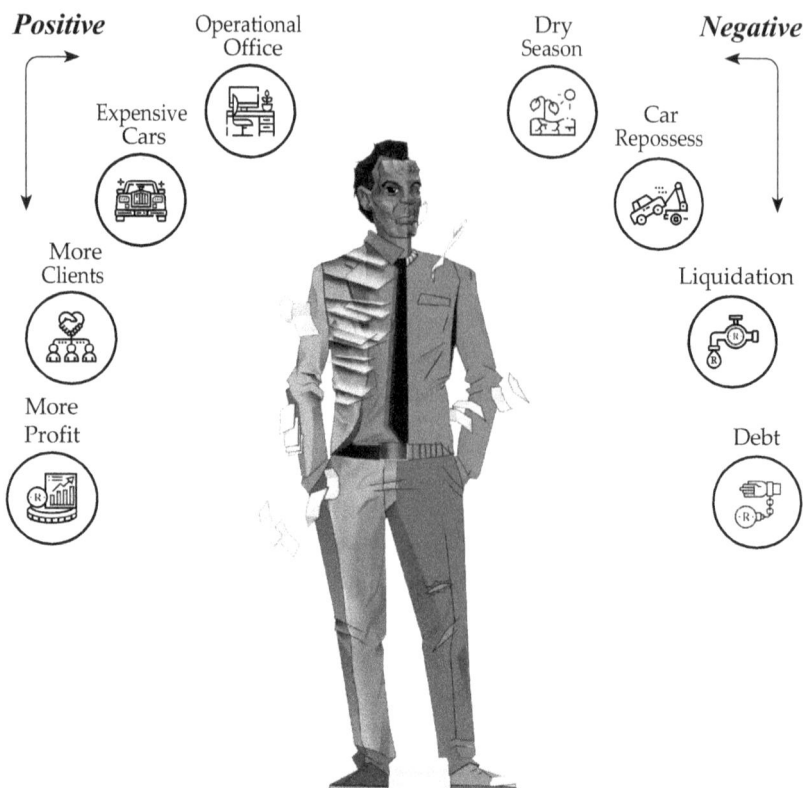

Figure 4: Mr Entrepreneurship
Source: *Author's own construction*

Figure 4 is the picture of MrE himself, what a complex man! Besides the looks, MrE has features that are difficult to describe then there is the process or the journey with you, let's talk about that as what is perceived to be the journey and the real journey are two different things.

"Mr Entrepreneurship" (The process)

MrE, when I started dating him this (Fig 5) is what I thought our marriage would look like, but I was so wrong. What I came to make peace with is you like attention, you want it all to yourself and success takes time.

Figure 6 is what our life or marriage looked like. I am convinced that a lot of people who have not dated you think dating or marrying you will look like Figure 5. It's time for a reality check, entrepreneurs!

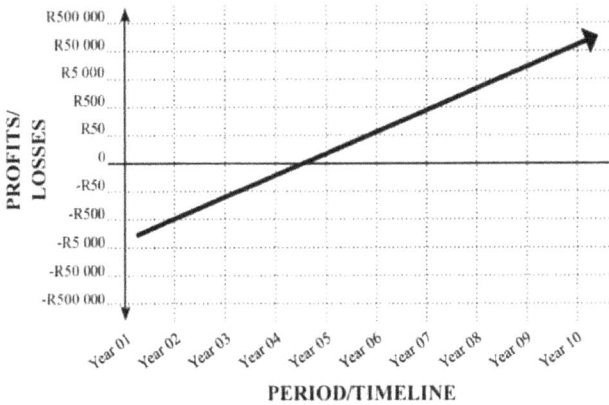

Figure 5: Perceived Entrepreneurship journey
Source: *Author's own construction*

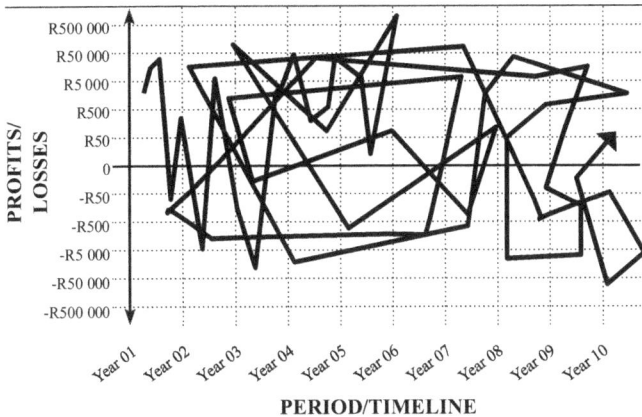

Figure 6: Actual Entrepreneurship Journey
Source: *Author's own construction*

The process is never straightforward and well-defined upfront but some of the things that will happen on the way is you will have lots of knocks before you get a breakthrough. Here is a process guideline, it should help you once you have made the decision that you want to date MrE, it's not a perfect process but it is a good starting point.

Entrepreneurial Process

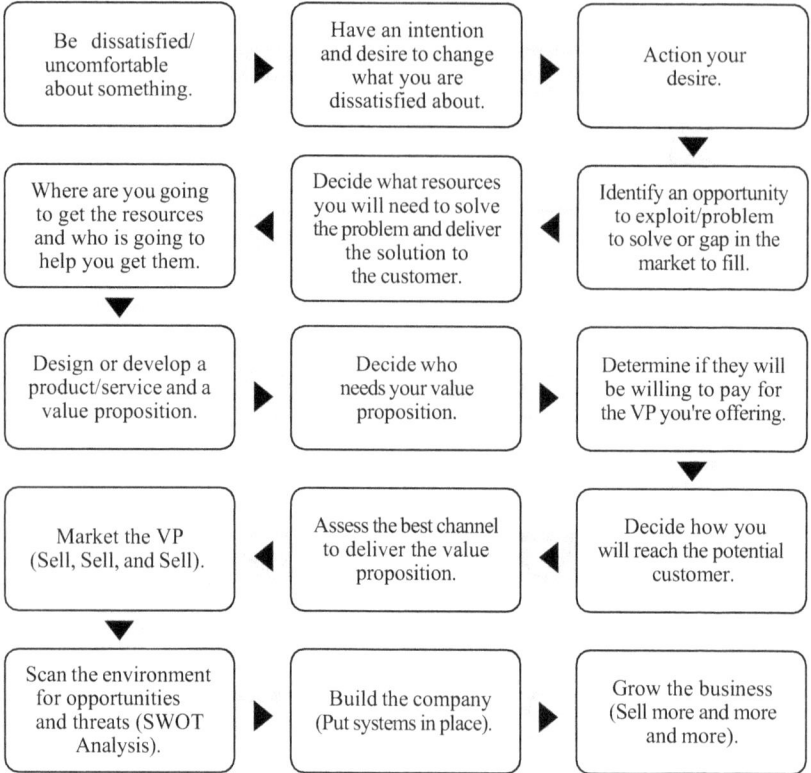

Be dissatisfied/ uncomfortable about something. ▶	Have an intention and desire to change what you are dissatisfied about. ▶	Action your desire.
Where are you going to get the resources and who is going to help you get them. ◀	Decide what resources you will need to solve the problem and deliver the solution to the customer. ◀	Identify an opportunity to exploit/problem to solve or gap in the market to fill.
Design or develop a product/service and a value proposition. ▶	Decide who needs your value proposition. ▶	Determine if they will be willing to pay for the VP you're offering.
Market the VP (Sell, Sell, and Sell). ◀	Assess the best channel to deliver the value proposition. ◀	Decide how you will reach the potential customer.
Scan the environment for opportunities and threats (SWOT Analysis). ▶	Build the company (Put systems in place). ▶	Grow the business (Sell more and more and more).

Figure 7: Simplified Entrepreneurial Process
Source: *Author's own construction adapted from literature*

Besides how you look like, the perceived and the actual process there is also the issue of how life will look like for MsE once she says, 'I do' and who really qualifies to be called MsE.

Ms Entrepreneur (The person/individual)

MrE, there is a big fight about who is a real entrepreneur and who is not. What qualities do you look for when looking for a life partner or don't you care (whoever feels can be your wife then you happy to take them)?

Here are some qualities that I have put together, based on what I have read, observed, and heard as we continue to wait for MrE to tell us the qualities of an ideal MsE. We are not going to discuss them in detail, but I am only sharing the list

25 qualities of Ms Entrepreneur: What must she possess?

How an Entrepreneur looks like or her life becomes after becoming MsE. The life she inherits by being MsE?

1. Alert
2. Autonomy
3. Balance (hands, heart and mind)
4. Big dreamer
5. Bounce back quick
6. Charismatic
7. Crazy
8. Energy levels on steroids
9. Fearless
10. Flexible
11. Good with building relationships
12. Heuristic bias
13. High level of achievement
14. High level of self-efficacy
15. Independent
16. Internal locus of control
17. Intuitive
18. Leader
19. Over-confidence
20. Over-optimistic
21. Quick decision maker
22. Risk-taker
23. Self-confidence
24. Unrealistic
25. Visionary

Figure 8: Ms Entrepreneur
Source: *Author's own construction*

How would you know you are a perfect fit for MrE? You need to use the qualities listed above to check what you have and what you still need to work on to qualify. Fortunately, you can learn or develop them. So you don't have to be a perfect fit you just have to be willing to grow old and wiser together with him.

But most importantly you need to know which marriage type will work for you before committing. Sometimes the only way to know is by trial and error but sometimes your context will guide you. Know yourself then know what is best for you. No one size fits all in entrepreneurship.

LETTER

3

A SUITABLE MARRIAGE CONTRACT

THE SIDE HUSTLERS AND FULL-TIMERS

Dear MrE

One big question that most people would like to get an answer directly from you about is which type of marriage guarantees success to anyone and everyone who chooses to marry you? When we talk about the different marriages in this context, it is generally referred to as side hustling/ part-time entrepreneurship, or full-time entrepreneurship where a person would devote 100% of their time and resources to make the marriage work. There are also those who are not interested in marrying you at all, they are 100% employed and devote all their time and resources to their jobs, they don't even dream of dating you for various reasons. The question though, is more about the first two types, the latter is not the focus of our conversation.

So far no one has been able to answer this question with 100% certainty and this is one of the things I am yearning to have a conversation with you about.

I wish I could look you in the eye and ask all these confusing questions; hopefully, you can answer these questions with more certainty, so that the level of uncertainty that comes with marrying or dating you is minimised, and the likelihood of success is enhanced.

With the above question, MrE, comes a big debate of who is a real entrepreneur, who qualifies to be called MsE? Currently, those who dedicate less than 100% time to you are not viewed as real entrepreneurs and are characterised as lacking seriousness. Is this how you feel, MrE? Does it matter whether a person is a side hustler or full timer? Would that affect the likelihood of success of the marriage? If not, what is it that will negatively affect the marriage, if side hustling has no effect?

Yours in Love
MsE

The wait for MrE continues and we continue to share our thoughts as we wait for him to respond to my letters. Let me start by sharing insights from three entrepreneurs I had a conversation with Dr Hajo, Ms Nthabi and Mr Mzo on their views and experience on side hustling and being a full timer. This is a conversation we had in one of the Wits Business school online evening dialogues in a quest to get different views on this matter in the absence of answers directly from MrE.

Case 1: Dr Hajo Morallane (Both an employer and employee – Side hustler)

Dr Hajo has been running her business while working for years. she has had an interesting entrepreneurship journey; her business came from her Phd in entrepreneurship assignment. Dr Hajo is a full-time employee and runs a hair manufacturing business on the side. She reckons her journey started weird, very different as she never imagined she would be an entrepreneur one day, she always thought entrepreneurs have it hard and she could not see herself dealing with that level of hardship.

"I was like this bright, young corporate climbing person, nope, it is not for me," said Dr Hajo, as she jokingly shared her sentiments. In her case, especially with her natural hair business, she soon discovered that she doesn't need to run that factory herself. While she is still employed, she decided to outsource the manufacturing to somebody else.

Dr Hajo gave a perspective on how she started as she was asked to answer the question "when is the right time to jump ship and go marry MrE full time?" and she said "for me, that time has not come" as she explained how she is managing it all because everything she does is eCommerce related. Dr Hajo continues to say, "I wanted to jump at some point to set up a factory until I discovered that there's another way of doing it. And yeah, that's my story to say when is the right time to jump? I think business will dictate to you when to jump and if you need to jump".

Then, Mr Mzo Gulwa and Ms Nthabi Mokgosi had a different story to share as they have already jumped ship, unlike Dr Hajo. Let's hear their story and the key insights that we can deduct from their experiences with the hope that it will help us decide if we want to marry MrE or not and if we do, what marriage contract is ideal.

Case 2 : Mr Mzo Gulwa (Side Hustler who has jumped ship to full-time entrepreneurship after 11 years of being a full-time employee)

Mr Mzo shared that he started his business (Purple Growth) as a side hustle after being with the bank for 11 years but intending to resign and be a full-time entrepreneur one day. All was well until the business started picking up, the expectation at the bank (MrEm) grew as Mr Mzo occupied a senior position. Additionally, he had a lecturing portfolio which was growing and demanding as well. "I just became overwhelmed, and I had to make a decision, I knew something had to give; I said to myself I can't do all of these at the same time", Mr Mzo continued to explain.

"It's great to have all of this money coming left, right and centre. But I had to decide because with time you realise that performance in some areas is suffering. And you will make both MrE and MrEm unhappy in the process while trying to satisfy two husbands".

You are only human and can only handle so much. I was one of those who received the Employee of the Year Award almost every year at the bank and also did reasonably well in the lecturing space, I was fairly a star everywhere. The portfolios were growing. I then said, No, no, no, something has to give. I decided to leave the bank in 2019, two years after starting Purple Growth. What I had done was to put a team in place to run the business on my behalf. What do you do when everything becomes average, and you can't make it your best because you don't have enough time? You have to choose. That's where trade-offs come in and I chose to go full-time entrepreneurship (I married MrE) while still maintaining my lecturing portfolio.

My main thought around this is to take your time. Take your time, don't rush to go in full time, it looks exciting and sexy when you look from a distance. It comes with a lot of credibility and praise, but life will humble you. Business will humble you. And once you've left the corporate space, remember, it's a bit difficult to get jobs now. Then you fail in business and want to come back, but the door is closed already, and no one can take you back because there are no jobs. You have to be very careful about this decision. Take your time, that's my approach. But also, the issue of trade-offs becomes essential because every one of these two options will have a benefit and a bit of a disadvantage. So, my view is, if you go the side hustle route to say, 'I remain employed', you are going to achieve and acquire less, especially in the short to medium term. Remember, if you are full time in that business, you could do what you do in one year in one month for an example, reminisces Mr Mzo.

Case 3 - Ms Nthabi Mokgosi– The digital boss (Side Hustler who has jumped ship to full-time entrepreneurship)

Ms Nthabi, who has a design business, added, and confirmed she had similar challenges. She started side hustling when she was still at varsity, designing logos for other students. While at varsity, it was working pretty well; the challenge began when she started a full-time job and ran her business at the same time. "So, it was a side hustle when it began. And then later on, I was fully employed, a fitness graduate and all that, and I was running the business on the side. But of course, later on, it caught up with me because as the business grows, you get an opportunity to get more clients, more services and more projects are coming. And if you have two jobs, it is not easy. At some point, I had to make a decision."

Ms Nthabi also brought in a critical issue of mental health which confirms what Mr Mzo said: "you are human, and you can only handle so much. So, it caught up with me when I couldn't juggle the two because I was sleeping less, getting sick and relying on energy drinks and all of those things. It became difficult for me to even focus, I think earlier, Mr Mzo mentioned that you know when you start underperforming, and it's not like you're not performing, but the fact that you are not giving it your all becomes a little bit tricky in that regard. If you're not giving your ultimate best, it becomes a problem and something suffers someway. I realized that too, and I thought about it, and I was like, I need to decide.

Now, we can never actually have a definite answer to say, when can I jump ship? Because with me, I jumped ship because I realised that I had to make a choice and I could not keep up. It was not like I planned that at a certain time I would jump ship, but time constraints and health issues were more push factors for me and I had to jump quick as all was not great anymore".

Tips and thoughts to ponder on before you jump ship from Mr Mzo, Ms Nthabi and Dr Hajo. Should people stay side hustling or jump ship and if they do, when should they do so?

1. Timing - Is it advisable to even be looking to leave work permanently in such a challenging economic climate created by COVID? Shouldn't one be looking at keeping a full-time job and then continue to side hustle for as long as possible? The truth is side hustling is a safer option but is a matter of tradeoff.

2. During high unemployment, don't rush; take your time because if you decide you made the wrong decision and you want to go back to employment, it might be tricky.

3. It depends on your business; some businesses you can easily manage remotely, but some you can't.

4. How fast you want to grow will dictate this.

5. Do you have a trusted team to manage your business while you are away?

6. How demanding is your full-time employment? Would you have time to do both?

7. Are you able to get human resources to manage the business for you while you work full time? If 'yes' work till you are financially stable to focus on your business without needing a salary.

The three entrepreneurs reckon that any marriage contract type can be good or bad as both have their advantages and disadvantages. Different individuals will prefer different models or marriage types. However, there are trade-offs and it's a matter of what you want to trade-off for and the decision is based on a couple of things for that specific individual which include but are not limited to: risk appetite, support structure, financial responsibilities, background, time constraints, type of business (more automated or hands-on) and is the business too reliant on skills from the owner or more outsourced.

Lessons learned about the two different marriage types

Should I side-hustle or jump ship and go full time and when is the right time? This is normally a question I get asked as a mentor, coach, and lecturer. This is a question that no one can answer for you, only you can. However, here are my thoughts, in addition, to the thoughts shared by the three entrepreneurs. You can digest these as you think about whether you should or should not.

Different models for different people, which model is ideal for your context? Be true to yourself

Consider your support system, time, and mental health, the demands of both worlds and your finances. Do this for both side hustling and jumping ship, what challenges you might have to deal with, and how you will deal with them. Write this down on a piece of paper and compare for yourself, use ideas from the tips shared here to answer your questions and calm your anxieties.

Be true to your context, don't compete with anybody.

Don't feel inferior when somebody says you're not a proper entrepreneur as a result of you having a smaller business or a side hustle. Find your model and do what works for you. Our situations are all different.

1. Whether you prefer to side hustle for life is your decision, there is nothing wrong.
2. If you decide to side hustle until at a certain point it's your decision as well; there's nothing wrong with that too.
3. Should you decide to say, "I want to be an employee, I'm not getting involved in entrepreneurship". There is nothing wrong with that too, that is still your decision.
4. All of us have an appetite for different things. We get fulfilled by different things so be true to your context, which is imperative. I always emphasize this because sometimes you find the belittling

that happens can put pressure on others to commit to a model or marriage type that's not suitable for them. Those who are full time feel they are better entrepreneurs than those who are hybrid. So define for yourself what is best, if you want to be a small business for life it's your decision, if you want to side hustle for life it's your decision too. But take a model or marriage that works for you and then you will be happy and enjoy it because it's what works for you.

Summary of the Pros and Cons of each marriage type

Side hustling advantages

1. Low risk.
2. Financial resources to fund the business.
3. Consistent income to cover the basic needs of life.
4. Have time to build the business without eating the seed because of basic human needs.
5. Have room to fail and learn.

Side hustling disadvantages

1. Limited time.
2. Employees have time to take advantage of your absence.
3. Less flexibility.
4. Employer policies and possible conflict of interest.
5. Work pressures may force you to always prioritise work deadlines and neglect the business thus missing opportunities.

Full-time entrepreneurship advantages

1. 100% attention.
2. You can do more faster and achieve a lot.
3. You can set up systems and develop a culture as you want it.
4. High likelihood of high returns faster.
5. Involved enough to recognise and cease most opportunities.

Full-time entrepreneurship disadvantages

1. High risk.
2. No fallback place.
3. Pressure to get to profitability fast.
4. Limited funds for growth at the startup stage with no cash flows to attract external funding.
5. You have to learn and this can increase the likelihood of costly mistakes.

Jumping ship for the wrong reasons

It is easy to jump ship for the wrong reason and in haste then forget to consider things that are important which can make your transition smoother. Wrong reasons to jump ship:

1. Your boss made you angry.
2. Thinking you will work fewer hours than at work.
3. Thinking you're going to be rich quick.
4. Peer pressure.
5. Seeing others looking more like celebrities, there are many other reasons that you might get out there and find out they are not as linear as you thought.

What do you consider when you need to decide whether to jump ship or to stay side hustling?

1. Consider your responsibilities timewise and financial wise.
2. Remember we all have 24 hours.
3. Consider your support system, who will take care of some of your responsibilities.
4. Make sure that you have enough money at least; if for example, you are busy saving as you are running a full-time job, make sure that you are secured because you don't want to get out and your business is suffering at the same time.

5. Employ only people you need to move the business forward while you side hustle, don't bring in too many people because you can't sustain that, it takes time to start seeing profits in a business.

The truth of the matter is whether you take the hybrid or the full time model, both of them have their risks, challenges and benefits. So you need to sit down and do that exercise, put your risks, challenges, and benefits down and do some tradeoffs, which one is going to work for you. No one is a better entrepreneur than the other, if side hustling is the model that works for you then so be it and if full time works, then so be it. Choose the model that works for you to be true to your context. But be true to your context. It's hard to balance two jobs so stay true to your yourself. Even if you are optimistic that you will make money tomorrow and support yourself, you must plan for the worst case scenario because you still need to eat while you are marketing and building.

Be true to yourself, you know your context better

To the Youth: If you are young and don't have financial responsibilities and more than that, you have someone who can support you financially when it goes wrong, that is a conducive environment for you to try something as you can afford to fail. Postpone big debts, kids and marriage if you can and allow yourself to fail without it negatively impacting too much on others.

9 things to do before quitting your day job

When you have entrepreneurship in your blood, the temptation will be great to resign from your job and go for it. The sensible thing, though, would be to make sure that you tick these boxes before you do, says **Dr Jabulile Msimango-Galawe**.

1 BE WILLING TO FAIL
Is there room for failure in your life? If you answered 'no', you aren't ready to be a full-time entrepreneur. You'll be ready when you can say 'yes' and accept failure as part of the process.

2 HAVE A VISION AND A PLAN
Your plan should entail the what, how, when and why. It will be a roadmap to your goals. Don't only plan the next two months; plan for the next three years and beyond. It won't be 100% accurate, but it will help you to land close to your target. Without one, you could land anywhere.

3 HAVE A BUSINESS MODEL
Don't waste time on a 20-page business plan; focus on a straightforward, quickly implementable business model. If your business isn't too complex, use Excel and do the essential financial calculations (profits, markup, break-even, overheads).

4 CHECK CONFLICTS OF INTEREST
Will your employer's policies, notice period and other legalities affect the products or services you built while in their employ? If you are going into the same industry with the same services and products, be sure that you are allowed to.

5 COMMIT TO LEAN STARTUP PRINCIPLES
Keep overheads low. If you don't need an office, don't have one. Downgrade your lifestyle so that you don't put too much pressure on the business. If you start out with a corporate mindset, you're bound to fail.

6 GET SUPPORT
There are only 24 hours in a day and if the business has to support you financially, you'll have to put in longer hours than nine to five. If you can, get an assistant, be it at home or in your business.

7 GET YOUR FAMILY ON BOARD
Talk to family members who will be impacted financially or otherwise by your decision, and get their buy-in.

8 BE OVER-OPTIMISTIC
You will need a healthy dose of over-optimism. The day you lose it, is the day you stop growing and stagnate. But watch out, it could lead to failure too.

9 FORMALISE YOUR BUSINESS
Formalise the company before leaving your job. Once you are operating full-time and professionally, you will need compliance documents to access funding or other opportunities. ◼

> Dr Jabulile Msimango-Galawe is the founder of DrJ Business Support, co-founder of the African Institute for Entrepreneurship and director of the Master of Management in Business and Executive Coaching at Wits Business School.

Figure 9: Nine things to do before quitting your day job
Source: *Old Mutual SMME Magazine Issue 1, 2021*

51

LETTER

4

PARTNERSHIPS AND OWNERSHIP - 100% VS. 0%

Dear MrE

The issue of ownership is a big and a very sensitive one, it goes deep into South African history of apartheid where only whites owned things and Black people worked hard to help them acquire and own as many assets or businesses as possible. As a result, ownership is a big thing that has spilt over even to this marriage with you MrE. There is a hunger to own, and it does not matter what the value is, we just want to own. Maybe let me qualify my statement and not generalise to an ambiguous 'we'. Most of us want to own and I am qualitatively using the word most, I don't have stats to back it up. It is based on my intuition, experience, and observations. In this letter, I hope you can answer the question of why ownership is important (if it is) and when getting married to you when does ownership of the "house" (business) become important. Entrepreneurs are hungry for 100% shareholding.

As I reflect on some of the things I wish you had answered in the letters I sent to you 6 years ago, I feel like your responses might have helped me make a better decision as to whether to own or not to own.

And if I chose to own what is worth fighting for and what is not worth fighting for. In 2010, I was faced with the issue of ownership of my then business. When my business was struggling financially, MrE, I sold 49% shares to a white company that was looking to take me under their wing as an Enterprise Development beneficiary. The agreements were clear - they would invest money in the business in exchange for a 49% stake and I would use that money to process orders and pay off some of the business debts and also help me cover overheads to avoid creating more debt. In that way, their business would improve their BEE scorecard and my business would be able to get back on its feet.

The conflict started when the ED partner wanted to bring in their friend who was in the same industry and business of supplying schools with learning material. Let's call the friend 'Oom Pieter'. Oom Pieter has been in the business for years and had a client base of mainly the white former model C schools that I had trouble penetrating; since Oom Pieter was a white person, he could penetrate that market and I had the Black township schools. Price is a big factor in the stationery business, or at least then it was, since I have been out of that industry for more than 10 years now. If both types of schools/client base were to come under one umbrella that would give us economies of scale, because wholesalers and manufacturers give their clients prices according to their buying power. That sounded like a win-win as that was going to improve our margins, and both Oom Pieter and I would not have to stress about cash to pay for orders, because of better cashflow as a result of improved margins and the cash injection from the ED partner.

Then we reached an agreement with the ED partner that Oom Pieter could join the business and bring his clients along to be under one business which I still owned 51% and the ED partner owned 49%. From the start, the understanding was clear that I would remain the MD and the majority shareholder of the business but when Oom Pieter joined, the ED partner wanted to change this around by making him the MD and allocating him shares.

I did not like that idea but when these discussions started, the implementation on the operational side had already happened and we were buying all stock using the accounts and credit lines of my business that I owned 51% of.

We had changed the signatories of the business bank accounts to include a representative from the ED partner, this meant that no transactions could happen without the signatories from both parties. But what we did not do was update all the supplier credit accounts to capture the new directors, so that we all took the responsibility for whatever happened according to our respective responsibilities as directors and shareholders of the company. I was the only one who signed surety with all the suppliers and never updated the signatures when the ED partner joined. Unfortunately, this meant that I was the only one responsible for all the liabilities of the business, however we all had access to the cash in the business bank account.

This was a big mistake which was caused by the fact that when I got into this partnership, the business was struggling, and I was desperate to get a cash injection and have cashflows. Focusing too much on getting the cash injection meant some important things fell through the cracks when setting up the partnership. And one of those things was ensuring that we were all responsible for the business liabilities when the ED partner joined.

I refused for Oom Pieter to get shares and be the new CEO of the business because I felt I started the business and I struggled enough for a long time alone why should Oom Pieter just come in to be the CEO and even own shares if all he is bringing is clients and the capital injection does not even come from him anyway. I was obsessed with owning 51% and being the majority shareholder but I did not do the critical analysis and the mental acknowledgement that reducing my share and getting capital in so we can continue to operate is better than owning 51% with no money to operate.

54

With the advice I received from friends who were thinking like me, things were bound to go wrong and fall apart. My closest friend and advisor at the time was Mr Nceba Galawe, and we both did not know much at the time, so it was an issue of the blind leading the blind. He gave me a lot of good advice though, but on this specific one we both allowed our emotions to get the better of us. The biggest lesson I learned is to watch out for where you source your advice, don't get it from someone who is emotionally invested in your business. On serious matters like partnerships, get objective expert advice. Secondly, when you ask people for advice or their opinion on an issue, never tell them your interpretation and feelings about the issue at hand that they are about to advise you on as that clouds their judgement and makes them lean more towards your perception of the issue. Describe what happened without adding your opinion and emotions into the matter.

Consciously or subconsciously, they are more likely to support your side of the story if you tell them a subjective and most likely biased story which cheats you out of getting valuable input that is objective. Thirdly, get advice from people who have experience, knowledge on the subject matter at hand so you gain from their wisdom and experience, but the fact that you ask for advice does not mean you outsource the decision making, you still have to make the decision but you open your mind to hearing a couple of options at your disposal, hear the advantages and disadvantages for each option and then at the end, evaluate what is on the table and make the decision. That's what asking for advice is about, rather than soliciting support for your subjective view and decision. That was the mistake I made, instead of asking for advice for that purpose I asked for "advice" which was generally saying help me implement this decision rather than help me see other perspectives, their pros and cons.

MrE, we could not agree, and this ended ugly. I ended up with 100% shareholding of my business that had negative value and lost an opportunity to reduce my shareholding so that I accommodate Oom Pieter as suggested by my ED partner, the upside would have been the additional client base that I could not access and the capital injection from the ED partner. Another benefit I missed is that Oom Pieter had years of experience in the stationery and school learning material industry and solid networks, particularly in markets I could not access. You see what was worse, MrE, was that I was left with a bank account I could not use and debt with suppliers that I could not service. It's like getting married in community of property and not thinking about the possible negative outcomes and being so desperate to get into the marriage that you do not make sure all contractual issues are properly covered so you are protected.

Yours in Love

MsE

Now let me talk to entrepreneurs, remember when things fall apart, the courts will look at your contracts and decide based on that. They won't take your word that the debt isn't yours and how you feel about paying the debt that you were sometimes not a party to. Don't rush, go through your contracts properly and get legal advice wherever possible. To summarise, the mistakes to watch out for when getting into partnerships or bringing in new directors and shareholders in your company.

1. Make sure the paperwork is done upfront and reflects the verbal agreements.
2. Don't be hasty to get the money out of desperation that you end up taking liabilities alone while everyone benefits from the upside.
3. Have a plan B or plan to leave in case the partnership goes sour.
4. Don't close all your exit doors because you might end up stranded.
5. Be open-minded and ask for a second, or third opinion if you feel your judgement is clouded.
6. Ask from experienced people, not people who think like you or have limited experience like you.
7. Have a long term view when you make partnership decisions.

The partnership did not work out because the ED partner was going to continue only under the condition that Oom Pieter owned 10% shares and managed the operations. As much as I felt 10% for Oom Pieter was not justifiable, in the long-term it was going to benefit me as the business could have continued to operate. The brand was known and respected already in Cape Town, and had big growth potential, it was strangled by cash flow and not enough clients. No one was level-headed, neither my ED partner nor myself was willing to compromise, unfortunately emotions dominated the discourse. The situation turned ugly and we ended up taking each other to court, but later tried to settle out of court because I did not have the financial resources to sustain such a bruising battle against a well-resourced ED partner, so I ended up walking away and letting everything fall apart, hoping for a fresh start.

Since the business had other directors and the bank account had other signatories, I could not trade with the same business. I had to register a new business where I could be the only director and so that I could trade freely without needing anyone to co-sign. Because the brand was already known, I had to try and find a name as close as possible to the previous one and do all the registrations and compliance from scratch. It was not easy to start afresh and because of the credit lines that were in dispute with the previous ED partner that I did not have money to pay, my credit record was ruined with the suppliers. I had to start buying stock in cash and that complicated a difficult situation even further. Cash flow was negative, and I did not have a facility with the bank to shore up the negative cash flow situation.

I tried to borrow money from friends and family to continue operating, but there were just too many problems to deal with, as such, the 'come-back' I was hoping for, was short lived. I owed everyone and anyone who knew my name and I could not pay them. I had to let my employees go and moved all my belongings out of the premises to my house in the middle of the night because the landlord had already threatened to lock the premises and attach all the assets as I had not been paying rent for some time. As the fights were going on in the background not much was happening in the business, and I could not cover my overheads, including the rent so we had to vacate the premises at night. The next morning when the landlord arrived to lock the premises and attach assets, the offices were empty, and we had gone missing. Not that I am proud of that act, but a girl had to do what a girl had to do, I had to survive.

This was year 2010/11 and I was left with only one driver and had to try to operate from a very lean startup principle. I did a few things to scale down to a lean machine, from seven employees to only one. I started working from home, no rentals, I sold three bakkies and was left with only one for the few deliveries that I still had to do. I continued to scale down as it was harder to get back to the level I was at before and I ended up being the only employee left with only the car I was driving.

At this point, I had no energy left in me, the stress was just too much to handle. The backwards and forwards with lawyers, and phone calls from creditors enquiring when I would pay them. Calls from clients wishing to place purchase orders and I did not have the cash nor credit lines to execute the purchase orders. It was madness, I could not stay sane, I was losing it and my health deteriorated very fast. That's when I started to have migraines and at the time, they were severe, I would just go numb when I suffered a migraine attack, it affected the business, my family and everyone around me. I could not operate anymore. I was a zombie walking in the streets of Cape Town. But I kept my smile, no one knew what was happening behind the scenes, except my closest friends and family.

I was a dead woman alive; I would be there in the same room with you but not be present. I had hit the lowest point in my life. I started missing MrEm and started questioning my marriage with MrE. It was dark, I had no hope, and I could not see the light at the end of the tunnel.

My entrepreneurial spirit was dead, there was nothing innovative or creative coming, and my brain had stopped coming up with ideas and ways to get out of the sticky situation. I was stuck, going back was far, as much as going forward seemed as equally far. I was at a crossroad and all as a result of choosing MrE over MrEm, maybe not, maybe as a result of making bad emotional decisions (As she pauses to rethink whether it was as a result of marrying MrE or her bad decisions). I did not even have money to buy myself toiletries, I was back to being a real child again, and I was a dependent with great ideas and qualifications. My husband, at that time, had to support me and take over all my responsibilities. I remember even my mother would send me money for toiletries. My self-esteem was dealt a big blow considering that I was back being a child again needing support for my every need. It was embarrassing, to say the least.

The most painful thing was telling my employees that I had to let them go because I could not pay them anymore, their salaries were always late. It was unfair to them. I still remember that day as if it were yesterday when I called them to my office upstairs and told them I have to close down, it broke my heart deeply knowing that tomorrow they would have no jobs and most of them were breadwinners. On the other hand, they contributed in some way to the fall, they were not without fault, but I was the CEO, and I was fully responsible and accountable. I was the captain, I had to make sure the ship did not sink but I failed to do that. I needed to push them to deliver and meet their targets, but I did not push hard enough; perhaps I should have let them go sooner? I guess we all paid the price in the end.

Everything just fell apart so quickly; the truth is, it felt like it was so quick but yet not so quick. I reckon the signs were there and red flags were everywhere, but I was too busy to see and even when I saw them, I was too slow to decide to call it a day or make the necessary changes.

1. In business, you have to keep your eyes and ears open.
2. You have to act fast - you can't be undecided.
3. You have to be willing to fail fast and cheaply, don't drag it too long - it will cost you a lot and will make you struggle to recover.
4. Don't only use your heart to make decisions, balance it with your head, and put some in-depth thought into it.

I can still clearly remember the first time I experienced how a dishonoured debit order felt like; a severe throbbing migraine pain, being overdrawn and summoned, relentless calls from unpaid creditors and I felt like I was losing my mind. On the same tone and breath, the first time I tasted a million, I grew the fastest, felt fulfilled with work, felt I was adding value and making a difference, had full control of my destiny, had flexibility and control of my time; was when I was in business. You win some, you lose some, but you can't avoid the losses, you have to go through it all to get to the other side cleverer.

"Life packages are delivered in pairs; you have to sign for what you did not order to receive what you ordered. You sign up for the failure to receive the success, that's just how life packages are delivered" DrJ

At school we were taught that success is to pass your subjects, the assumption is that learning has happened when you have passed your subjects. In entrepreneurship, success is to fail, you must fail to pass. To do well in entrepreneurship, you must fail, the learning happens when you fail, unlike in school where the learning happens when you pass. How do you change that mind-set so that you embrace the failures in entrepreneurship, such that you learn and get on the other side wiser and a better entrepreneur?

Entrepreneurship: *To pass is to fail and to fail is to succeed.*

School and Life: *To pass is not to fail, to not fail is to succeed and move to the next grade.*

The compounded effect of mistakes will lead to failure and failure will lead to success. No one knows the absolute equation or formula for entrepreneurship success; it is too complex to explain and describe on a one-dimensional piece of paper using the current vocabulary that we have at our disposal. Whatever you are told leads to success in entrepreneurship is not absolute and the story is incomplete.

Dear MrE

So how do we make it work if it is so complex and this was the answer I hoped to get from you, MrE? Additionally, how important is ownership and what trade-offs does one have to make. MrE tell me, from what I shared, can you see that one of the factors that can have either a negative or a positive effect on an entrepreneur's business and lead to failure or success is partnerships and shareholding. I hope while we wait for you MrE, that entrepreneurs will apply themselves properly when they get into partnerships as that can complicate or simplify their lives. We hope you will share more wisdom on this issue soon.

Yours in Love

MsE.

LETTER

SOCIAL CAPITAL
CORRUPTION OR NETWORKING

Dear MrE

This is my fifth letter to you, I hope you had a chance to read the previous four letters I sent to you, so when you get the time to sit down with me to have a conversation, you would have already read and prepared to answer my questions and share your views on some of the things I wrote about you which you might find interesting. I am looking forward to a sit-down with you, I am excited, and I can't wait to meet you face-to-face. The fifth issue I want us to chat about is the issue of corruption and social capital. It is always difficult to differentiate between the two as when you talk to people from the public sector, they seem to refer to what the private sector refers to as social capital as corruption. It has left me confused and I would like to hear your thoughts on my understanding of this issue. Here are my thoughts, about which you can correct me and bring some clarity when we meet. I am not a legal expert, I am not going to talk about the legalities around corruption but only a perspective on effectively using social capital while conscious of what is viewed as corruption and the grey area between the two.

Corruption and networking are the two terminologies which bring confusion and I believe they need to be understood for them to serve us well in this marriage. Misunderstandings and unrealised expectations can break a marriage. If the other expects you to use social capital to make the marriage work while the other feels you are a corrupt person when you do that, the conflict is bound to have a negative effect in the long run. Corruption is a very deep word with legal implications; in this book, we are not going to go into the legalities but use the word carefully.

Yours in Love

MsE

What is the difference and how is it relevant in this marriage? But before we try understanding the differences, let's conceptualise and understand social capital and its benefits. In entrepreneurship studies, we teach that social capital is like an asset for your business. And one form of social capital is networking, but at the same time, we need to watch out that we are not found to be corrupt, practising nepotism or being unethical while we try to extract benefits and privileges from our networks.

Research-based definitions vs. perceptions on social capital and networking

Social Capital: It is operationalised through networks. Relationships and networks from which individuals can derive institutional support. It entails actual and potential resources accessible through an actor's network of relationships. Social capital creates value (privileged access to intellectual, financial, and cultural resources) and provides a platform to access opportunities. One of the dimensions of social structures is social relations and within those relations, some gifts and favours are exchanged. This is what social capital means and the benefits are embedded in it. Does it sound like corruption; how would you define corruption if it sounds different? Social Capital Theory explains the ability of actors to extract benefits from their social structures, networks, and memberships. It means knowing the 'right' people – those people who can help you achieve your goals.

Business networking: It is the process of establishing a mutually beneficial relationship with other businesspeople and potential customers and suppliers. The primary purpose of business networking is to tell others about your business and hopefully, turn them into your customers[14].

The benefits of networking and the risks of overvaluing networking

I have seen the value of social capital. Unfortunately, because it does not make it to the balance sheet we can easily take it for granted or think it is a nice to have. It is a necessity, a very important element in the business that can give you a competitive advantage and moves you forward faster than you would under normal circumstances. Since social capital is operationalized through networking, who you know matters. If you are an entrepreneur you can't build relationships just for the fun of it. You need to have those that you build for purpose with a bit of conviction. Don't just go anywhere, go to places where you know you might meet and connect with people that will be of value to you.

At the same time don't take for granted any relationship, you never know what you might need when. No one succeeds alone you need people to succeed and those are the networks you need to build. Network with a goal in mind, have a bigger vision than drinking beer and making jokes with people you spend time with. Don't get me twisted there is time for beer and jokes but as an entrepreneur don't let that make you miss an opportunity that is sitting in front of you. Entrepreneurs never switch off from being entrepreneurs you have to always be sharp and your mind must always be searching for opportunities and something that will improve your entrepreneurial journey.

(Tehseen & Sajilan, 2016)[14]

You need to be intentional about knowing people in the right places. Unfortunately, in South Africa, sometimes this matters more than your business idea if you are looking to get access to the market and funding in certain places. We shy away from saying it most of the time, but it is the reality of the business world. You can have a good idea but if you don't have anyone who can help you through the process and open doors for you, your idea might not make the cut because of limited resources. This is truer for the Black child who has no rich dad or uncle to give him or her startup capital and link him to networks that can allow him to succeed. We (me and my friend Nceba) normally refer to the entrepreneur who has no chance at accessing certain opportunities because of not having social capital or not knowing people in the right places, *"Sipho Dlamini"*. Don't ask me why *Sipho Dlamini,* I don't even remember how we arrived at that name.

This does not mean it is always the case, there are a "lot" of people who start with just the idea with no networks but in cases where you need the networks, you better have them ready than be found wanting. Entrepreneurs have a perception (might be a fact) that if you are *Sipho Dlamini*, you have no or very low chance of getting tenders and funding from certain institutions. Where do I get this? Because I mentor entrepreneurs, I teach entrepreneurship, and this is where such perceptions get shared. Because I have access to so many entrepreneurs, I get to hear a lot about what happens in the space more than just my own experiences. And most *Sipho Dlamini's* have even stopped applying for funding from the institutions that have come to be known to be funding only their friends and families or funding only those that they can benefit from one way or the other.

What is the solution? If others have them that means you can build them too. I hear what you are thinking. How? The same way you built the ones you have now but going forward do it with a bit of focus and intention. The ones you have now might just be social networks, but they were built in one way or the other, so you can build the business networks too.

I hear you ask, is this ethical getting funding and tenders because know someone? If you have a good business idea but you can' funding because you have no relationships with people, then build t relationships. That's all I am saying, build strategic relationships networks that will help you get resources for your business. Trust you need it in South Africa!

Unpacking the how and some tips

When I entered into business in 2003, I had no business networks were aligned with what I was doing. The networks I had were not us for business purposes and I knew no one in the right places so I slo but surely started building relationships with a bit more intention focus.

This is what I did:

1. I joined relevant organisations and forums (Example: Busin Women Association (BWA), South African Women's Netwe (SAWEN), Cape Chamber of Commerce, etc.)

2. I started attending networking events where there would relevant people and I made sure I was active and not just in background.

3. I looked for businesses that were in a similar industry to and started connecting with owners who were open to relationships and collaborations.

4. I looked for white business owners who were looking to s black and women-owned businesses (Both sides looki similar things, I needed a white company that was trusted a to penetrate the market and the white company was also for a black company to comply with BEE and to penet "black market"). I call these mutually beneficial relat with reciprocity. This is how I learned about the clothing and gifts industry by working with someone w the business already, especially in the promotional item My intentions were clear that one day I would run my

independently once I had learned and we were both fine with it. After I left, we did some projects together on a collaboration approach rather than a fully-fledged partnership.

5. I attended trade shows and workshops, etc. my intention was not just to enjoy the workshop, but it was to talk to people and start building relationships. I am an introvert, so you can imagine how much that took out of me but I had to get used to talking to strangers, as uncomfortable as it was.

6. The organisations where I was a member, I did not just sit and keep quiet, I made sure I was visible, I served on committees and built friendships to make sure I was known for something, known for delivering value.

7. I entered competitions and built relationships with other entrepreneurs as well, I made sure I got their contacts and kept in touch.

8. I started a soccer tournament as part of giving back to the community where we operated (Free State, Eastern Cape, and Cape Town) and this created a platform to build relationships with existing and potential clients.

9. I volunteered and offered my skills for free to organisations like Shanduka, the national mentoring movement mentoring entrepreneurs. These platforms allowed me to meet more people.

10. I also volunteered to be a judge in one of the township entrepreneurs' awards in Gauteng which resulted in me being a judge on two TV shows (eTV and Mzansi 1 Magic). All these made me visible, remember the rules of the game, numbers bring business.

All these paid off, cold calling became less as a result of networking. Referrals started becoming the rules of the game. We would refer each other when someone was looking for services which we knew someone from our networks could help with. For those who had been referred to me, I made sure I gave them a satisfactory service, then word-of-mouth became the order of the day. In some relationships

you might not see immediate value from them, and sometimes for a number of years, but one day you get shocked that the person you met 10 years ago is now in an influential position and you can use your social capital.

More than just receiving, networking is a reciprocal game, you can't just receive one way. It's a give and take, so you can't be self-centred, you need to show your network that you care about their needs too and not just yours. In that way, you build long-term, lasting, value-adding relationships.

The rules of the networking game are

1. Be visible
2. Add value and care about others too
3. Be trustworthy
4. Reciprocate
5. Be known for something
6. Be consistent
7. Be professional
8. Don't be a parasite
9. Be intentional
10. Be patient

DrJ Entrepreneurs Breakfast (For Learning and Networking)

"Building Strong Meaningful Business Relationships"

Because I value social capital so much; when I became a resident of Johannesburg I started my own networking platform. This included breakfast sessions, a Facebook group and a WhatsApp group. The objective of the breakfast sessions was to create an environment conducive enough for entrepreneurs to build strong meaningful relationships while learning from each other's experiences over breakfast. It was a face to face event when we started and we moved from hosting one event a year to hosting Quarterly but we had to pause because of COVID restrictions. A few months after COVID restrictions and lockdown we decided to start an online version of it.

As an entrepreneur when conditions change you must always be prepared to change, flexibility is key in the game of entrepreneurship otherwise if you don't move with the times you will be dead in no time. A lot of entrepreneurs waited for things to go back to normal until their businesses could not be revived anymore. Time is money in business, you can't just wait; you have to pivot fast and start operating with new or revised business models. Though we were flexible to move online it was never the same as it lost that human touch which was a unique selling point. We received good feedback about our sessions both online and face to face as relationships were built and entrepreneurs had a place to connect with like-minded people and unwind, more than anything else share their experiences and learn from each other. It was also a platform to showcase their products and services and try to get new customers.

My advice for entrepreneurs is to find yourself a group with whom you can network and build relationships and it will come in handy one day. Just remember the rules of the networking game.

Social capital through the lens of a society mired in corruption

An important consideration when we talk about social capital and using your networks to access resources and get favours that you would not have acquired if you did not have relationships with the right people in the right places, is the thin line or grey between social capital, corruption, nepotism, and ethics. I am no expert in these concepts or subjects, but I must mention that they can be confusing as these are socially constructed and mean different things in different contexts or countries. Sometimes they can mean different things in the same country, depending on whether you are in the public or private sector and also on the person who is assessing your actions.

The reason I am bringing this up here is because I don't want you to be caught unprepared or found wanting and then try to plead ignorance because that might not fly. Educate yourself on these concepts so you stay clear of trouble. If you do business in different countries, get an understanding of that country's norms and beliefs, as what is deemed corruption or unethical in South Africa might be perfectly acceptable in Nigeria, France or any other part of the world and vice versa. Social capital is an acceptable business term in the business world but what becomes a consideration that I want you to keep in mind is the operationalisation of this concept as that is where the confusion and differences come in.

Let me make a practical example based on my personal experience as I have done business in both the public and private sectors. In the private sector, I captured most of my business or clients through networks. Someone will say they are looking for a statistician to conduct some data analysis and then someone from my networks who knows that I am a statistician will share my name and the potential client contacts me and we talk and I get the business. This is called social capital because I accessed the opportunity via my network and networks are a form of social capital.

Whereas in the public sector if you do exactly as I stated above, you might be accused of being corrupt for giving business to your friends. You have to go out on tender or solicit three quotes before you give someone business. It can get very confusing when the businesses that tender have some kind of relationship with any of the officials inside, then those businesses are likely to be disadvantaged which is the opposite of what one would get in the private sector. They might be denied the opportunity to participate as that might be deemed corrupt that they get business while someone they know is working for that institution. In the private sector, your networks, the people you know, help you access opportunities but in the public sector that can hinder you from participating in opportunities.

I must say I am not naïve to the fact that the use of public money has to be managed differently from private money, and also knowing of real corruption that has taken place. Is it justifiable though, because it is having unintended consequences for those who have relatives and friends employed by the state who are honest business people and they are disadvantaged in the process? Someone can argue that is not what is happening to the friends and families of people in the public sector, especially politicians who are benefiting unfairly, they have taken it beyond social capital to corruption. All I am trying to bring forth is for you to be aware of the differences and interpretations of the words 'social capital', 'networks', 'ethics', and 'corruption' so you behave as expected in the different contexts.

The real corruption that has been happening has somewhat made life difficult for the friends and families who want to do honest business with the public sector, note the keyword 'honest' business as we know there are those who use those relationships to do dishonest business.

My advice is to know the differences between *corruption and social capital* in different contexts. Social capital is not an unethical or corrupt thing but can easily be if you don't know how it is viewed in different contexts and countries. Corruption in the private sector vs. corruption in the public sector might be understood differently, be careful not to get trapped. Always try to be ethical in the way you do business even in a world where being unethical seems like a norm and more of a systems issue than we can dare to admit. I know I am bringing in a different concept, but this goes hand in hand, as corruption usually emanates from there. Ethics are moral principles that govern a person's behaviour or the conducting of an activity. Have some values that guide your behaviour, and, in that way, you will be able to stay clear of unethical behaviours which might lead you to corrupt spaces. Values - principles or standards of behaviour; one's judgement of what is important in life. In ethics, value denotes the degree of the importance of something or some action, intending to determine what actions are best to do or what way is best to live or to describe the significance of different actions.

I hope the definitions and explanations will give you something to work on when deciding what is it for you and what is it you plan to stay clear of, so you are not found wanting.

L E T T E R

6

FINANCIAL SUPPORT

Dear MrE

To warn you upfront, this is my 6th letter, and this is where I vent unreservedly to you. This is where I spit it all out as this is a frustrating issue and this is where most entrepreneurs feel let down by the government institutions and agencies tasked to play a role in filling the gap that private sector funding or banks have left uncatered for.

Access to funding: Why is it so difficult to get financial support in South Africa? Access to funding is always at the top of the list of factors that hinder entrepreneurs from succeeding. Nothing seems to be changing, the more announcements about funds being made available to SMEs, the more the challenge of access to funding remains top of the list. MrE, this can't go on like this, we can't always be complaining about funding - when are we going to stop complaining and start receiving the support and attention we deserve.

Unreasonable requirements: *When are the requirements going to be relaxed so they reflect a risk profile of a real SME or startup which is highly risky by its very nature? When are the requirements going to take into consideration that most Black people come from an era where their parents had nothing, no riches, no property, no assets, nothing? All they had is their sweat, sweat from working for white people who paid them peanuts so they can stay poor. After that, the generation that is trying to start businesses is asked for collateral, credit records, cash flows, balance sheets and the likes. Tell me where would a person who worked and was paid peanuts get all these things? Whites can be asked for all these things; their parents will provide collateral on their behalf or sign surety. Tell me where a black SME will get all these things from? If a young person went to study further, she probably studied using loans and parents had to take those loans to take them through university and now the young Black person wants to start a business and you ask for collateral. The collateral likely to be obtainable is the sweat from working for white people and debt created to make up for the monies they were never paid for their sweat. The collateral Black people have is debt, which I dare to say, if they were fairly compensated for their sweat probably, they would not have accumulated the debt.*

Why the unreasonable requirements: *What makes it worse is when the developmental financial institutions (DFIs) that are mandated to fill the gap by catering for this market of Black businesses trying to start something new or have new ideas come with the same ridiculous requirements. My sense when I read most of these requirements is that these institutions wrote the requirements as if they were meant for a corporate with resources, a history of 100 years of trading, and owners coming from a wealthy background. SME funders are looking for low risk (corporate type of risk) from an SME which is risky by nature, and they won't find such which means they won't fund SMEs that need the funding.*

The bad attitude of employees meant to service entrepreneurs: Besides just the unreasonable requirements, there is another frustrating issue, the attitude of the practitioners or employees hired by the funding institutions that are meant to service entrepreneurs and help them through the application process to financial close. The attitude is just not one that says we are here to support you and make your journey easier, we know being an entrepreneur is hard enough as is and we are not going to add to your stress by delaying the process, not responding to your applications or taking donkey years to approve your application and disburse the money. There is no urgency in most of these institutions, employees are just happy to be collecting their salaries and go home every day without even successfully processing one application. My question is, why practitioners?

The employees don't care about funding entrepreneurs as much as they do about getting their salaries, a null hypothesis I wish and hope to be untrue. Researchers should examine the kind of attitudes employees who are meant to service entrepreneurs have and why. Perhaps have former or failed entrepreneurs occupy these positions that are meant to serve entrepreneurs. Individuals with a passion for entrepreneurship not hobbled by a corporate mentality and poor understanding of business risk.

We can't fund you; your business is risky. It's called entrepreneurship, if you take the risk away then it is not entrepreneurship funding anymore. The funding criteria that looks for corporate qualities in an entrepreneurial venture. Who is fooling who?

Just to paint a picture for you of how bad things are out there, let me share some findings from a study I was involved in which was done by Finfind during the lockdown concerning funding during that time. This statement by no means suggests that there is nothing good happening, but this is my effort to highlight what we still need to pay attention to and improve to find ways to navigate the financial support space.

Finfind's 2020 report on the impact of lockdown and COVID- 19 found that one of the biggest challenges entrepreneurs encountered when trying to access funding was receiving no responses to their applications. And from those that received responses more than 90% were rejected and reasons stated included bad credit record, collateral and more . More than 60% of entrepreneurs reported access to funding as their number 1 challenge. For a more detailed report visit the Finfind website.

Who should be appointed to support entrepreneurs? This is a serious issue that requires those who employ people who are to serve entrepreneurs to reconsider the selection criteria. What kind of people are ideal for servicing entrepreneurs. Do you just check qualifications and then appoint them and hope that they understand the complexity of entrepreneurship and the urgency of entrepreneurs? I think more than just the qualifications, people who are employed to service entrepreneurs should be a special breed who have the personality (People's person), entrepreneurial understanding and background and drive to make an impact. Not corrupt practitioners looking to get a share from every deal brought to their attention and certainly not greedy individuals. These must be people who understand how important entrepreneurship is in growing the economy and how imperative that growth is to all citizens in the country. It might be worth considering people who were entrepreneurs who may have started something in the past and failed as they will understand the pain of waiting for funding until the business closes down. All of these do not guarantee anything but improve the likelihood of getting desirable outcomes and having less money sent back unspent when there are so many entrepreneurs needing this money to make a difference. Enough with the venting, let's flip the coin and look at this from a different angle.

I am convinced that money is available but those who are supposed to be dispatching it just make it difficult to access it because of the requirements and no sense of urgency from the funder's side, worse even, the unclear requirements and mandate of each institution also just exacerbate the problem.

Do we really need funding at the level we think we do or is it just a perception: With money difficult to access or should I say perceived inaccessible MrE, the question is can we start and get this marriage going without money and keep it healthy and sustainable without it especially if the owner comes from the Black race? And if we get the money does that mean our problems will be solved and we are bound to be sustainable and successful? The song making the rounds is money, money, money, money, and money!!! It's all about the money or is it not? Are other people being held back by access to funding while they can do it by themselves without the external funding but because they are focused on external funding they miss the opportunity to be innovative and make it work without the external funding? I know this won't be a practical solution for all kinds of startups but some can definitely benefit from bootstrapping and having a DIY mindset when access to funding is the problem, as this boils down to accessibility vs. availability and how big the need is.

I always ask this question to force my fellow entrepreneurs to start thinking about Plan B, "what else?"

What would you do if no one wanted to give you funding, would you close the business, give up on your dream or are there other options at your disposal to go around this?

Sometimes we think we need money to be happy or to make our marriages and homes happier, but we overestimate what money can do for us and what we can do with it. By no means do I want to trivialise the role money plays in our lives and how much easier things can become if you have access to it. But that does not stop me from cautioning everyone that it is not always about money. The wisdom is in knowing what needs money, what doesn't need money, when you need money, why you need it at that time and what you can do if you are without it. So here wisdom and innovation come into play big time as without money one needs to be creative on how they will make it work and bootstrap their way throughout.

We can't give up on our dreams just because someone does not want to give us money or is not convinced we are thee deal to give money to. So you need to start saying "ok they don't want to give me money, so what is the next practical thing that I can do?"

Let me use an example to illustrate that when we don't have money, it is easier to think it will come and solve more than it really will. I talk to ladies sometimes about marriage and money matters in marriage and if they would opt for partners with money or without money citing certain challenges that come with each. Those who have husbands with money but are unhappy in their marriages claim they would all rather have a man without money who treats them well and they will be happy while some even left their husbands with money because they were not happy. Those who have husbands with no or little money say I would not mind crying in a mansion with lots of money to do what "I need to do but I can't stand a man who has no money and I cry twice (no money plus treated badly)" so some leave because of that. If you analyse these two statements you will note the common denominator is happiness.

The ones with money leave because they are not happy and the ones with no money also leave because they are not happy. So money or no money the outcome is still the same, happiness! So the money does not necessarily address that part. And this brings me to my argument that maybe in your case it's not money that you need so desperately, it's something else and the question is "have you done that analysis to assess how much external funding you need and if you can do without external funding?" It's not by default that access to money will make your business work, it can fail with lots of money so you need to be careful of not exaggerating the need to access funds.

Therefore, I say again, in marriage, it is not always about the money but we need and want money for other things and when we don't have it, we think if we possess it; it will soothe our pain and address our unhappiness.

This is the same in entrepreneurship, MrE, we overestimate the need for money until we get it and fail while having it, then we realise it is more complicated than money. Money can make it less complicated, but can't fully uncomplicate it.

During the early stages of my first business, I could not get funding from any institution as I had no cash flow to show, no collateral to mitigate risk and no credit record linked to the business. I applied for funding and was declined so many times. At some stage, I got my breakthrough and started getting support and approval in different forms (skills development, marketing material, and prizes from competitions which I did not have to pay back as they were grants. I also had various forms of funding like loans, overdrafts, lines of credit, invoice discounting and many more).

Since I was still in my youth at the time these were some of the places that I managed to get help from by either receiving the funds or having certain invoices from suppliers paid for using vouchers: Masisizane-Old Mutual, FNB Invoice Discounting, 40% Purchase Order Loans, Umsobomvu vouchers, The business Place, Technoserve and SABKickstart. Some of these funding types were the first time I heard about them like invoice discounting factoring but I was always looking for better ways to manage cash flow and take care of my costs and in that process, I learned a lot of things on the types of funding that were out there. Most of the private sector funding only kicked in later as I could only qualify when I started having cash flows and profits to show.

As you can see, I had multiple sources for financial support and this excludes my savings from when I was employed, investments I made while working which I had to withdraw to use to build the business, and the personal credit and overdraft facilities that I had. I had all the money, but the marriage still fell apart. I must emphasise that as a startup I could not get any of these. I started getting this kind of support after I had been running for a while and there was a cash flow to show to the funders for them to start funding me. In the early stages of the business, be ready to bootstrap because that is when it's difficult to get financial support.

I was once invited to SABC as a guest to talk about the challenges of SMEs in South Africa and here I took the opportunity to emphasise what I think is critically more important than access to funding. Let me share a bit about that interview and I hope it will give more supporting evidence on what I am trying to highlight.

A conversation with Ms Martine Solomon on the SABC Currency Morning show, discussing "some mistakes entrepreneurs can learn from and the top three things that entrepreneurs desperately need" What if it is not funding you need but a client or skills or something else?

What are the common mistakes that you have encountered as a business person?

Mistake 1: Not understanding the industry

I went into that business without understanding the industry, so I didn't do my research. I just looked at it and I thought, okay, not much capital is required as startup capital so I went for it.

Mistake 2: Not understanding the pricing and margins

I didn't understand the margins, I didn't understand the input versus the output or the amount of energy you need to put in just to get a profit of one Rand (R1). That was one of the big mistakes I made.

Mistake 3: Misunderstanding competition

I wanted the business to be professional, so I looked at other guys running stationery businesses from the back of their bakkies. I didn't want to be like those ones. I wanted to be professional, so I looked at businesses like Waltons (a giant stationery business) and other big stationery retailers and I told myself, I'm aiming to get to their level. I started by positioning myself in the middle between the back of the bakkie type of business and the big giants. But I didn't understand that there was a reason there was nobody in the middle. There you tend to fight with both sides (competition from both angles).

You have these small guys that are competing on price, they can cut costs as much as they can; you try to compete with them. And then you have the big folks that get big discounts from the wholesalers and manufacturers, you have to fight with them as well. So, in the middle, you find yourself a bit stuck and it can be difficult to make profits and be successful.

Mistake 4: Failing slow and expensive

Yeah, the thing is, it was a big loss for me, and a very painful one. You know, they say when you start a business, the guaranteed thing is that you are going to fail. What you have to decide is whether you fail cheaply, or expensively. I failed very expensively because I ran for a long time at a loss and that cost me a lot of money and that didn't sit well with me. As much as I closed the business, I asked myself a lot of questions, am I that stupid? I related failure to stupidity at that point. I also asked myself, if all these people were stupid because the stats are damning, it is like 90% of people who start businesses fail? I wondered what it was that made 90% of people fail? I wanted to figure it out. This is when I decided to register for my PhD. I hoped that in the end I would be able to come up with a logical assessment that informs the 90% failure rate, but what I found out was that nobody knows the answer in the entrepreneurship world. We just have to feel our way through, right? asked Ms Solomons. Exactly, it's literally fail fast, fail forward and fail as quickly as you can, and then dust yourself off and just try again.

I know that you have started DrJ business support and this is a solutions business for small businesses within South Africa. Please tell us more about your business.

In 2015, I decided to start again, the business was called JoyG business services and because of my role at Wits, students started calling me 'DrJ' and then DrJ became popular. I rebranded the business such that I can run with one brand. So now, it is DrJ Business Support and mainly focuses on supporting entrepreneurs, professionals and post grad students.

Based on what I have learned when I ran my first business; sometimes we make stupid mistakes because we don't have somebody else who has walked the path, similar path, and a person who can guide us along the way. That's when I decided to start DrJ as a mentor. While continuing with mentorship I learned a bit more about coaching. I then realised that mentorship sometimes has its limitations. I introduced coaching as well and changed my model to a blended approach. For entrepreneurs, the mentorship with a little bit of coaching works best whereas for professionals and executives, coaching works best and sometimes a little bit of mentorship. I find that model works very well in supporting entrepreneurs and professionals alike.

Top 3 needs for SMEs, funding can come as the 4th need in most cases

In your opinion, what are the top three things that entrepreneurs desperately need?

Interestingly, funding always comes top of the list, I failed with funding, I had the loans, the overdrafts and the grants but I still failed.

1. **Market access:** What I think should be top of the list is market access, 'you need a customer'. You can have all the funding but if you don't have a customer, it is not sustainable.
2. **Entrepreneurial skills and business acumen:** You need training and an understanding of what you are trying to do. So you need that entrepreneurial skill and business acumen to understand what is and what is happening.
3. **Financial literacy:** you also need more than just getting funding, you need financial literacy so you understand your numbers and you can manage your finances better.

If I can just recap what DrJ has said: The top three things that entrepreneurs desperately need are definitely not funding, but a client, training and development and then most importantly, financial education, which is so critical for every entrepreneur.

That's the top three according to me and is subjective, but research has also shown that these are key for when you get assessed on your funding application.

As much as I have illustrated that it's not always about funding, it is still important that the funders play their role so those who need it can access it with ease. The mystery that embodies funding in South Africa needs some serious attention from those in authority. "SMME Funding in South Africa is a mystery that funders like to keep mysterious and a mystery that entrepreneurs long to see demystified".

Tips and advice to funders and entrepreneurs:

I had an online conversation in 2021 titled "SMME funding in South Africa during covid and beyond" where I talked to people who work in the business development support space either as researchers, funders or in enterprise development during one of the Wits Business School evening dialogues. We have to hear their thoughts on what can make the funding space effective and I believe this will be useful insights to any entrepreneur thus my decision to include it in this book and share it with you, it's available on YouTube as well if you want to watch the full conversation.

The COVID-19 pandemic has brought significant challenges to South African small, medium, and micro enterprises (SMMEs). In response, both the public and private sectors have provided much-needed relief funding for SMMEs as a stop-gap measure.

SMME funding has always ranked as one of the top items on the list of SMME challenges and usually when you listen to speeches made by government, the narrative is that there is a lot of money set aside for SMMEs but when you talk to SMMEs, they say access to funding is one of the biggest hindrances to the growth of their businesses. Some questions remain unanswered, and we should have those uncomfortable conversations in search of practical solutions to SMME funding in our country (South Africa), especially in times like the COVID-19 pandemic (This conversation took place in 2020 when SMMEs were struggling due to lockdown and restrictions on businesses).

Have the requirements to access funding been relaxed during this difficult time? How effective have these interventions been? What needs to change to ensure ongoing support for small businesses and startups going forward?

To answer these questions, we had an online conversation with a panel of experts from the funding and entrepreneurship space. The one thing that was explicit in the conversation and comments from attendees was that something needs to change and needs to change quickly as we cannot continue using the same criterion that was developed years ago when times have changed so much, worse is that the requirements are mostly unchanged even during COVID-19. It is evident, that the criterion we have is not helping in optimally serving entrepreneurs' funding needs, entrepreneurs will tell you that they can't access funding while funders tell you that funding is available. Clearly, we are not talking the same language and we are not on the same page, thus the need for a change and a review of what is not working and how it can be improved so we can achieve the country's economic ambitions of job creation, poverty alleviation and reducing inequality, which is partly expected to come from the SMME sector.

These were some of the matters raised during the online conversation and need to be reviewed:

1. The employees that are meant to assess SMMEs – do they have a clue what kind of animal an SMME is or are they looking for a big corporate in an SMME, are they just ticking boxes with no context, what is their attitude towards funding SMMEs?

2. The risk profile of an SMME is not the smaller version of a risk profile of a big corporate and those who assess SMMEs need to be educated about these differences

3. The gap between the expectation from funders and the realities of SMMEs (capabilities) need to be closed if we are to move forward

4. When you ask a Black entrepreneur for collateral when s/he is looking for funding to build a big business, what are you asking for (Collateral tends to be a white privilege in the South African context). How is this requirement helping us in dealing with inequality?

5. Working in silos (integrate the funding system with a non-financial support system for effectiveness. Each node in the ecosystem should feed into another

6. Financial Education: funders need to educate entrepreneurs about funding types and requirements and their mandates must be public information and clear

If the funding space in the country is to be optimal, change needs to happen from all angles and all stakeholders in the funding or entrepreneurship ecosystem need to play their part and be flexible to change.

First what needs to change on the supply side (funders):

What do funders need to change?

1. Communication – Funders need to send out clear messages and be honest about their requirements and what they are prepared to fund or not fund.
2. Transparency - This means advertisements with broad criteria that leaves entrepreneurs guessing needs to change and have specifics. The way risk is calculated must be public knowledge, why all the secrecy if you want entrepreneurs to come ready?
3. The funder's mandate must be clear and not a secret wherein entrepreneurs only get told at the end of a long process (submitting a lot of documents and waiting for months).
4. Risk appetite of funders – Funders of SMMEs in South Africa are very risk-averse, including public entities (DFIs). The challenge we would like to put to the government is for them to play an enabling role and help minimise the risk for funders to make it attractive to fund risky SMMEs. For example, things like collateral asked from a small entity owned by a young Black entrepreneur should be something of the past. Stats show that Black people, especially young entrepreneurs, have no collateral so why ask for it if you want to fund them?
5. There is a gap in the market in funding smaller amounts or micro-businesses and the question is how can the government make this sector attractive and de-risk it a bit?
6. The process needs to be simpler, and funders should interact with entrepreneurs.
7. Non-financial support is needed but can't be a one-size-fits-all and used as a scapegoat for funding SMMEs (i.e., unending non-financial support, entrepreneurs never being funding ready even after going through all the training stipulated in the beginning).

8. Other ways of reducing the need for loans and overdrafts etc. is to pay entrepreneurs on time (It should be a crime to pay SMMEs late) and buy from SMMEs. If they have clients, their need for certain types of funding will diminish, risk decreases, and they can focus on growth funding.

Overall, the requirements in general, need to be reviewed. Unrealistic requirements like asking SMMEs for audited financial statements need to come to an end. Even now during COVID-19, we are not winning and one of the attendees felt very strongly that channelling relief funding to the banks was a big mistake as banks are not flexible (They have stringent rules and applicant must have a good record with the bank and skip so many ropes before they can get funding).

What do entrepreneurs need to change?

Entrepreneurs sometimes don't cover themselves with glory as they lack some of the things that are within their power to have; things like keeping records and making sure they are always prepared so that when they need funding, there are a few things to work on towards qualifying. This was one of the pieces of advice given by one of the panelists "prepare for growth in advance and make sure you keep a record of all important documents". Entrepreneurs need to:

1. Get financial education and training.
2. Build a track record.
3. Ensure compliance (CIPC, UIF, VAT, Tax Clearance etc.).
4. Understand the criteria.
5. Have good financial record keeping, including management accounts, and receipts of all expenses, etc.

The outcome of the session was a way forward which is that private and public funding institutions need to come together and have a conversation with small business owners, incubators and other organisations representing SMMEs on innovative solutions on how to address the issue of access to funding in the country which has been on-going for too long. We are not where we were 25 years back but the fact that access to funding still tops the list of entrepreneurs' challenges, suggests we have not moved much. We cannot continue with business as usual and keep talking over each other; we need to come together to make access to funding simpler and easier.

Funders need to reflect; what are those unnecessary requirements that small businesses will never be able to meet and take those off the list. Equally so, SMMEs alike need to say, what are those requirements that are within their power to meet and start preparing themselves earlier on, so they are funding ready. The business support stakeholders need to work together so that it is all integrated as a functional ecosystem. Funders should not work in silos if the ecosystem is to be efficient, incubators can get entrepreneurs funding ready, and funders must focus on different stages and types of funding needed so we do not have a gap where you find everyone funds the same size SMME and no one wants to fund a particular SMME size or stage.

Moreover, it is not only about the money, but entrepreneurs also need to build relationships as networks can be useful in certain cases (i.e., collaboration). Additionally access to the market and paying SMMEs on time can also lower the influx of certain types of funding as entrepreneurs will have cash flows to run their businesses and only need growth funding and other types which are not a result of not having enough customers and late payments.

Thank you to the panelists for sharing their views on funding issues

- Ms Robyne Erwin – Mentor and Project Manager at Finfind
- Mr Grant Prince – SME Investment Readiness Manager at FETOLA
- Mr Phuti Mojela – Business Development Officer at NYDA

LETTER

COACHING AND MENTORSHIP

Dear MrE

This coaching and mentoring thing - do I really need it to understand how to stay married to you. Is it a must have, can I make it without using any? Can I just hit the ground running by myself and not have a coach or mentor and still win as best as I would have if I had a coach? That's another question I long to hear the answer from you about. While I wait for our conversation, MrE, let me unpack this by starting from the big debate of whether entrepreneurs are born or made.

Yours in Love

MsE

Are Entrepreneurs born or made?

First, to be born an entrepreneur means while you were in your mother's womb, your entrepreneurial characteristics were being developed as your body was developing into human form. What develops in the womb and how is a big question to answer. Before we start the debate of "born or made" research has shown that you become an entrepreneur by doing, it's a task-specific phenomenon, you do then you become. For me, that sounds like saying "you learned to speak and walk while you were in your mother's womb", but I believe you did not, as much as you needed all areas of your early development to develop fully so you were ready to pop out in nine months and later start talking and walking, it does not necessarily mean you were talking and walking in the womb, but you were born capable to learn and develop to a walking and talking baby. You watch people talk and walk, you see and hear, someone helps you through the learning process and then you start walking and talking. Same with entrepreneurship, you were born ready and capable to observe, learn and develop into a fully-fledged entrepreneur. It's not accidental that more people become employees than employers because that is what they mostly get exposed to and they observe, learn and develop into being fully-fledged employees.

What you mostly expose yourself to, you are likely to become consciously, subconsciously, or unconsciously inclined. There is a school of thought that entrepreneurial traits are genetic but that is another conversation for another day, which at the moment I do not have empirical evidence to support or falsify but it needs deeper contemplation on what makes an entrepreneur an entrepreneur, and how much of that can be genetic and how much of that can emanate from just pure exposure (learning, observing and repeating what you saw, learned, and used to build a belief system from).

The reason I am spending time driving this point home is because I don't want anyone to write themselves off that they are not born entrepreneurs therefore they don't have a chance of being successful entrepreneurs because "everyone" is born capable and ready to become anything they want to become. My emphasis is, don't underestimate exposure, it builds your belief system. It moulds you into something, as long as you are exposed, have observed, and have learned then you are likely to become what you have consumed. Also, you have an opportunity to take up mentorship or coaching to polish up some entrepreneurial skills, characteristics, beliefs, self-confidence, and entrepreneurial self-efficacy to be the best entrepreneur that you can be.

You are made by schooling, observing, learning, and repeating what you have seen and learned, whether being an entrepreneur, employee or employer. The truth is you are made, not born an entrepreneur.

Entrepreneurs are said to be born with this entrepreneurship thing in their blood. Do you know the analogy of soul mates? Is it true that when people are born, they have a specific person called a soul mate to whom the universe will connect them, no matter what? Does this mean irrespective of what one does, where she goes with whom she hangs around, eventually she will bump into her soul mate? I would love to hear what MrE thinks, and we will wait to have that conversation with him.

I, for one, think there is no such and anyone can be your soul mate, you just have to be wise enough to have a strong intuition to know when one is compatible, and you can do life together. Exposure is so powerful that when you get exposed to certain things when you are very young; you're most likely to confuse it with being born with it. Only to find out you have been exposed very early that you can't even remember when you started portraying certain characteristics, because you can't pin down a date when you started to feel, be and behave the way you do; you assume you were born with it. I have tried to follow kids who start showing love for entrepreneurship or some trait at a very early stage and adults who claim they were born being a certain way, when you follow closely, you realise they were exposed to things early on and they were not even aware that those things were shaping them to be the person they are today. When you are exposed, and you observe certain behaviours at a very young age, you will grow up to portray some similarities to your exposure.

Same with MsE, I don't think anyone is born an entrepreneur, but I think people get exposed to it early or later on in their lives that's why it tends to be correlated with how you were raised and when you were exposed and what you took from that exposure. Anyone can be MsE, marry MrE and live happily ever after.

But since it is not a birth thing but rather a matter of exposure, developmental and learning notion, it is therefore key that one gets a coach or mentor. In this way the entrepreneur can learn from the exposure and the experience of the mentor. This is the process of the entrepreneur "being made" rather than "being born" (coaching and mentoring process that's where you are made and of course, with many other factors that contribute to that process). Early exposure that made you be like "this" can be confusing to you being born like "that".

Being made by exposure, training, observing, mentorship and coaching

The question though is, do entrepreneurs really listen to their mentors, coaches, and advisors?

This question takes me to a concept of over-optimism where entrepreneurs feel and think they know, and this is because they over-estimate themselves. I think the over-optimistic nature of entrepreneurs makes them not listen as much as they need to, as they feel they know what they are doing and that their intuition is telling them 'it is going to be ok'. It does not matter how bad things look or what their coaches, mentors and advisers say, they believe they see better and that better is not as risky or as negative as pessimistic people are saying. They perceive anyone who shows them risks as pessimistic and not seeing the bigger dream or vision.

I think the analogy of side chicks explains this concept better. Sorry, I am going to use side chicks to explain this. I know most people don't like them except the husbands who date them of course. But there is something we can learn from side chicks. Those who might take offence in using the word 'side chick' bear with me, no disrespect or judgement is implied in how I use this analogy. I am using the term loosely as it is understood very well in our societies and is ideal to explain this marriage between MrE and MsE's optimism.

Entrepreneurs are like side chicks, they believe that whatever is happening to the wife of the husband they are dating or whatever pain is inflicted by the husband to the wife will never happen to them.

They believe the husband who is currently their side dude will treat them differently and better when they finally get to marry them and become the main chick/wife. They see what is happening to the current wife as something that will change when roles are reversed, and they are the wife. They are so optimistic that it will never happen to them and they will never be treated like that when it's their turn to be 'the wife'. According to them, the reason the current wife is treated badly is because of her doing and nothing of the husband's doing. So, whoever advises them contrary to their belief, they won't listen and that's how entrepreneurs are. The butterflies and 'pink love' make them believe and see positives and opportunities only, so they see no impossibility. Even if 90% fail/divorce or get treated badly they believe they fall under the 10% who live happily ever after.

The question is whether it's even worth it to advise entrepreneurs as they live in their own world where they don't want to think and acknowledge that sometimes things might go wrong and make plan B. Sometimes when you are not ready to hear what your mentor says and digest it, you won't benefit from the mentoring. It is not always the case that they don't listen, sometimes they are just not ready for it. Mentorship that is given to you, but you don't think you need is not that effective. Corporate ED providers should make sure their entrepreneurs understand and have a conviction about having an advisor before allocating a mentor to entrepreneurs they are supporting. Mentorship assigned by the ED or funder can sometimes be tricky as the interests might be different.

The ED might need you to create lots of jobs, but you might want to keep it lean but because you need the funds or support you have to accept the Terms and Conditions (T's & C's). I always say I wish I had a mentor when I started. I did not have mentors until later on as a result of the ED support I was receiving, which required the mentees to have mentors.

(In case you were wondering about the contradiction, in some cases I say I wished I had a mentor but now I am talking about the mentors I had). I only started using mentors later in my entrepreneurial journey, thus always saying I wish I had a mentor.

I had mentors, which included an entrepreneur, an executive at a bank in London, a retired CFO, an ED practitioner and many more. They were very supportive but sometimes I would not listen as much as I should have. Some advice was too corporate and was not implementable, and it was not their fault, but it was the best information available at the time. Sometimes, the key performance areas of the ED required the mentor to direct and advise us in a certain direction which was not necessarily my preference, but if you take the grant and accept the T's & C's then you have to comply. And most of the time you can't change the T's & C's nor can you reject the funding because that's all you have to get moving. Let me share some of the things my mentors advised me on and tried to help me with to make my business run smoothly.

Mr Wajdi Abrahams (contracted by SAB Kicksart 2008 - 2010)

Mr Wajdi was our mentor during the SAB Kickstart competition, he trained us on business planning and a lot of other things so we could be ready for the competition. He taught us about pitching and what to focus on when writing a business plan. He was a fantastic gentleman, very passionate about supporting us and seeing his region win the competition. He did a good job, so much so, that three of us went on to be nominees for the national competition and one fellow from our region, Mr Ashley Uys, won nationally.

Mr Wajdi kept saying 'sis' you need to tighten your belt, it's going to get tight with this recession and things are going to get worse before they get better. He made an example of my sales reps, "you are paying them a lot, you need to start cutting the benefits as the sales are not coming at the rate that you need them to sustain the salaries you pay".

I was over-optimistic, and I said no, we will survive, things will come around soon. I was also using my heart in my decision not to cut down their benefits as they were failing to meet their targets so I needed to have a conversation with them to start giving them an ultimatum and cut down, but I did not. Guess what, it got tighter as he said, things did not come around as soon as expected and the recession felt like it took forever. I hoped the recession would be over soon and sales would recover, I did not study the trends of how long recessions normally take and what happens during that time. I just followed my heart without the facts or research.

I paid dearly, so this answers the question "do entrepreneurs listen to their mentors and advisors?" In my case yes, I did but sometimes I felt like they were pessimistic, and I was over-confident. But remember, this is one case, many other entrepreneurs might share a different story based on their listening or not listening where outcomes were different. What I am trying to drive home is for you to apply yourself when you get advice, don't just be dismissive but at the same time don't just accept it as the absolute truth. You need to apply yourself and make informed decisions. Wajdi, my brother, I am forever grateful for the time we spent with you, it was a learning and growth phase for us, and you were such an easy mentor to engage and bounce ideas off.

Ms Benna Van Der Merwe (Masisizane ED practitioner)

She was the person I worked the closest with and was assigned by the Old Mutual Masisizane fund to me. She was very good, very passionate about what she was doing, she celebrated with me and would be disappointed when things were not going my way. She became an extension of the business, always willing to assist me. We tried all sorts of things to get me out of the woods and get customers. I had received a loan from Masisizane but the access to markets remained a challenge. The loan was specifically for purchase orders, but my biggest stress was overheads. I needed to get a big customer or many customers who could buy consistently so I could cover overheads.

We tried to get Old Mutual to procure from my business as their ED beneficiary and did not succeed because Waltons had a price advantage already so I could not beat them as I was assessed like everyone else (no special treatment because I was their beneficiary) so it had to make financial sense to Old Mutual, I had to compete with the big boys. So eventually they retained their existing stationery suppliers and the struggle of getting customers continued until I could not continue anymore. As a result of no consistent customers, I started struggling with loan repayments. Since I could not find funding to fund debt, I needed a customer to generate profits so I could repay loans, I needed clients who would be consistent and spend a reasonable amount of money. This is the reason I said earlier that one of the top three things entrepreneurs desperately need, is market access.

You need a customer; it does not matter how much funding you have if you have no customer, you will finish the funds and still die anyway. I know someone can argue that even if you have a customer, if you don't have funds to process the customer's orders you will still die. That's true but the reality is that it's easier to get funds for processing purchase orders than to get funds for overheads with no client to guarantee revenue. Benna, I will never forget how available you were and how much you wanted me to succeed, the fact that we could not get me into the database as a supplier for Old Mutual was not a reflection of you as my mentor, but the requirements made us compete with big boys and we could not beat them and this was outside your control. I know how much you tried to get those who had the powers to make the decisions to see our side of the story, but it was just not our day, but we prepared a solid business case - if all were equal, we would have won. Thank you.

Mr Gareth Pike (Old Mutual retired CFO)

Gareth was a retired CFO who came back to Old Mutual to give his time and give back to entrepreneurs. He was a very knowledgeable gentleman and it was easy to ask him all the finance "senseless" questions that I could not comprehend; like asking a CFO the finance 101 questions.

I wanted to learn so I asked all the senseless questions. There are a lot of things he advised me to implement in my business as financial controls and management, they made things easy and helped me to track and monitor what was happening financially in the business - the losses, the profits, the negative and positive cash flow. One of the pieces of advice that I could not implement was the advice on paying all my expensive debt as it was costing the business a lot and as much as it was good advice, it was not practical to implement because I was bootstrapping; there was no money to settle the expensive debt. Secondly, no one was willing to give me cheap debt. I had to continue taking the expensive debt (high interest rates) with longer payment terms because the cash flow was not healthy. In this case did I not listen to my mentor? I did, but I just could not implement some of the things because as a small business I did not have the financial resources that would allow me to make such decisions or implement such things. Thank you so much Gareth, the amount of time you dedicated looking at my financials, advising me and teaching me the financial lingo and key ratios to pay attention to made me understand financial statements even though I was a non-financial person.

Ms Wen Si (Cherie Blair foundation for women)

Wen was based in the United Kingdom and this was my first experience of online mentorship, we engaged using emails, WhatsApp and did our meetings via WebEx/Bridgeline. Because Wen was working in a bank and our meetings were during her office hours, we could not use video so everything was audio. She would set up the line and I had a code and a free line to dial in and that's how our sessions were conducted. It was such an experience to be coached by someone of a different race and culture and even of a different language, even though we communicated using English. I remember this was between 2016 and 2017 and I was busy finalising my PhD and she would read some parts of my PhD and advise me on some things that did not make sense, especially the part that I wanted to commercialise into a risk assessment App for entrepreneurs.

I developed that tool with her guidance, and she even bought me a book about entrepreneurs' personality traits, strengths, and types. This was a value add indeed in both my business and PhD studies. Thank you, Wen, for all the time and consistent follow-ups to ensure I keep up to my plans and goals.

I completed my mentorship programme officially in 2017 from Cherie Blaire, but we continued with our relationship for a while until I was comfortable that the tool was sound. Unfortunately, I was stuck when looking for funding to commercialise it and I decided to put it on hold in 2017. At the time, developing apps was not as easy and cheap as it is now and I was looking for something that needed a lot of controls, I can say a bit more academic on what the tool needed to do in the black box, it got expensive so quickly. The good news is that I am revisiting that project and looking forward to getting it in the market to assist. It is a tool that is meant to objectively assess the risk of entrepreneurs, their potential, and areas of development to focus on when going on an enterprise development programme or something similar. I will always treasure my time with you Wen, it was a value add and thanks to Cherie Blaire for creating such a platform for women.

All my mentors were great, but I was working against time, they came into my business when the green had moved to red, and it was crunch time. It only made sense that after being a mentee for so long, it was time for me to return the favour and be a mentor. I understood what being a mentee was like; I think that made me be a better mentor than I would have been if I had not experienced how it feels to be mentored. I have been a mentor and I have been a mentee; I have been a coachee, and I have been a coach and I continue to practice as both a mentor and coach. I have unique experiences and skills from each, which is what makes me understand things from both perspectives and that's valuable in my practice and journey of being an entrepreneur, lecturer, researcher, mentor, and coach.

DrJ as a mentee/coachee and DrJ as a mentor/coach

What I have learned from being on both sides of the fence, you can't walk it alone and expect to be at your maximum potential. We all have blind spots; we get lazy sometimes and we feel demotivated and struggle to hold ourselves accountable. And that's where mentors and coaches come in. Unleashing your full potential and helping you identify blind spots. My advice to you is get a coach or a mentor but don't dare walk it alone, it is not worth it, and the question might be, should I go for a coach or a mentor and which one is ideal for me?

A coach or a mentor: What should I choose?

As much as these two concepts are used interchangeably, they are not the same, they have commonalities, but they are different. They are both about a relationship and supporting another individual to grow, perform better and be at their best but they are unique in context and certain focus areas. Let's define each of them and see the commonalities and differences

Mentorship: This is a relationship between two people and generally the mentor has the experience, skills, and resources that the mentee feels she can benefit from. The context can be a career, business, personal or any other. The expectation is that the mentor must know more and have experience in certain areas that the mentee does not have. General practice is that, if one is an engineer, physiotherapist, pastor, teacher, or whatever profession for an extended number of years, they will take on a younger, less experienced individual to mentor. The mentees will benefit from the mentors experience, knowledge, and skillset. This is meant to minimise mistakes and speed up the growth process, instead of figuring out everything by yourself and bumping your head against the wall several times before getting it right, you have someone helping you to learn faster and progress faster than you would on your own. By the way, this can also happen in group settings where a mentor mentors a couple of individuals at the same time.

One thing that seems to be contradictory in entrepreneurship is that as much as you need to be an engineer, for example to mentor an engineer or be an accountant to mentor an accountant this does not seem to necessarily be the case in the entrepreneurship space. Here, it seems anyone and everyone mentors entrepreneurs, even employees who have no idea of what this entrepreneurship animal looks like. Is this a bad thing? Yes or no.

Yes, because an entrepreneur encompasses a lot of professions under one umbrella, as an entrepreneur you have to be an accountant, salesperson, manager, human resource, operations, technical, etc. And if you have an accountant who is an employee with the technical skills, you can still learn from them, but you just need to be able to know when the advice provided is too corporate and not applicable in your case.

No, because sometimes if you are still a novice in entrepreneurship, you can easily get misled into corporate approaches to your startup and that might kill your business faster than you can say the word fast. Worse if you have a mentor who is not humble enough to accept that he has no clue about the dynamics of a startup or small business but has only technical skills to share with you. In such cases you are free to have a second mentor who has walked the same path, who can guide you specifically on the complexities and dynamics of entrepreneurship and SMME.

Coaching: Coaching, on the other hand, doesn't necessarily require the coach to be an entrepreneur or in the same profession as you but they must have been trained to be a coach, they should have coaching competencies. So coaching is a relationship between a trained individual and a coachee and the objective is to support the coachee to be the best she/he can be, i.e., set goals and achieve them. Generally, this tends to be within a formal corporate environment and the focus is likely to be on professional development but some of that starts from personal development and then cascades down to business development (i.e. leadership, career, manager, employee performance, entrepreneurial performance, etc.)

Coaches normally define themselves according to their focus areas like a life coach, leadership coach, career coach, divorce coach, entrepreneurial coach, etc. When you look for a coach, then you select according to your focus area.

As much as coaching is about a trained coach rather than a coach who has experience in the same profession or discipline, most coachees like to select coaches according to their experience as people feel more comfortable with people, they feel understand their plight.

If you are looking for experience in your field when you feel you have no clue on what to do and where to start, you go for a mentor but if you are looking for coaching competencies to facilitate a process of becoming the best you without necessarily having to learn or draw from the person's experience then you choose a coach. A coach facilitates the process of development by asking you questions, challenging your thinking and what you do and probing until you find within you the answers that will unleash your full potential.

The other part is that a trained coach can be both a coach and a mentor, if you want both from the person then you look for a trained coach who has the experience or has achieved something that represents your ambitions, this way you will benefit from both the coaching competencies and her experience in the specific field.

For example, I am both a coach for professionals, managers, executives, entrepreneurs, students, and anyone who needs coaching, but I am a mentor only in the areas I have experience in, fortunately, I have experience in all the above listed. I can change hats and be both. In my practice, I use coaching, mentoring and a blended mentoring-coaching model as I assess and see which is ideal for which situations and then I apply the best method to give me the results the client and I require.

Not all good men are good for you, some are good for others so choose wisely

If you have never had a coach or a mentor in your life, try it and you will never regret it, but make sure you don't just pick but select according to your needs, so you don't get disappointed because of a mismatch. More than selecting a coach or mentor based on their expertise, you need to make sure that the chemistry is there as well, you need to understand one another, otherwise it will all fall flat irrespective of how good that coach or mentor is. Choosing wisely is like choosing a husband, not all good men are good for you. The same applies, not all good coaches and mentors are good for you; you know your type and if you get the match right, you will achieve amazing things and it will be effortless.

LETTER

8

THE VALUE PROPOSITION
WHAT MARRIAGE PROMISED ME

Dear MrE

Value Proposition! Value Proposition! Customer Centric!

MrE, what you promised me and what I received were two different things. Were you intentionally dishonest with me because you knew that if you told me the truth about the value proposition I was not going to be interested? Did you want me so badly that you were willing to get me to commit under false pretence?

All I knew was that it felt right marrying you but as to what that would entail, I did not put much thought to it. I just wanted to be with you but what I missed was that feeling right was not enough, I needed more because the feelings sometimes leave you alone to fend for yourself, at that point I needed more than feelings to sustain me. Feelings have a shelf life, they can't be relied on and sometimes they are moody, they are here today and nowhere tomorrow. This is how I feel, MrE, and hope you can shed some light as to what exactly the value proposition from you to MsE is and why most are not living happily ever after.

The value proposition you put on the table sounded like this: I will love you till death do us part, I will take care of you in sickness and in health, in riches and in poverty, for better and for worse. I was over the moon, I had a husband who promised to love and take care of me, no matter what, as long as I live. In my head, I was sure I would not struggle even for a day and that you would always be there taking care of me. But I was in for a big surprise, the road got rocky and I wondered if this was the same husband I chose, the same husband who promised me heaven and earth because it seemed like he was not even delivering the earth.

Was marrying you a mistake? The value proposition that you promised was very attractive, it was enticing. You were different from all others I had seen before MrE. However, what I found out in the marriage is that what was promised is not sitting, waiting to be grabbed. There are things I had to do to get the value and there are things I did not like to do but needed to be done if I were to enjoy the full benefit of our marriage and derive full value. Though not guaranteed that doing everything on my side was going to deliver the heaven and earth I was promised in its entirety.

When it started everything was spontaneous, it was just flowing or at least I thought it was flowing and I just went with the flow. It was butterflies all the way. I was feeling you and you were feeling me and it was evident that it is going to be a happily ever after story. But it was just the honeymoon phase, and the demands were not that strenuous until the honeymoon was over. The demands kept increasing and were more and more demanding, but the benefits were not increasing at the same rate (It was low and slow) and I was in a hurry to see it happen, to stand and to represent the #couplegoals and show that our marriage, MrE, was working. But was it working? The Value Proposition, was I getting what I was promised, or did I miss the small print on the terms and conditions? But everyone looking from afar thought we were on the right track, we were successful and life was happening for us, and that we had arrived.

The truth is, when we got closer, it started feeling and seeming like that but later it changed to something else as the foundation and the mistakes we made in the beginning were just too fatal.

Yours In Love

MsE

This marriage narrative can well explain two scenarios, first is a scenario where an entrepreneur (MsE) leaves full-time employment (MrEm) to marry MrE or start entrepreneurship on a full-time basis. The entrepreneur starts out excited, thinking she will be rich soon having seen others look like they acquired their success overnight so the entrepreneur is sure that she will also get her overnight success soon too. But she gets there and realises it is a long, lonely road before you get your big break. What the value proposition promises, lacks the details on what one will have to go through to get to the overnight success. Similarly, with marriage, people get excited about the wedding, the honeymoon, the butterflies and tend to forget about the real journey of marriage that involves two adults with their well-defined and established beliefs, values, morals, habits, behaviours, weaknesses, and the likes which mostly won't just be a perfect fit from heaven, there is work to be done to get to the ideal marriage.

The second thing this narrative reflects is a story of an entrepreneur who promises clients something and when clients get closer, start feeling that they are not getting what they were promised, and let's see if we can learn something from the Value Proposition MrE promised MsE and use this to learn and understand the game better. This is to avoid customers feeling cheated, when customers start feeling cheated, they won't come back and will tell others (word of mouth principle) when that happens, your marriage with MrE will get strained and start falling apart. Deliver exactly what you promised or at least more but never less. Never over promise, you rather under promise.

Let's talk to entrepreneurs or business owners and managers
Value!! Value!! Value!! Value!! Value!! Value!!

What is value? Being black/BEE, youth, and a woman is not a value proposition, you need to deliver more than that. Add value and you will see magic. Find what frustrates people, find the most severe pains that people would be willing to pay someone to help them get rid of, because it is too much pain to live with. Keep your eyes and ears open, listen to what inconveniences and frustrates people, then find opportunities to solve those problems for them.

Create value and be clear about what value you are creating and for whom; know exactly how much it costs to create that value. Know what you stand for: Quality, Cost-effectiveness, convenience, experience, newness, status, creative designs, etc. Know what it costs to produce your Value Proposition (VP) so you can know your breakeven point and your best profitable point and more importantly, your value destroying point which is when you go lower than cost.

Don't let negotiations for discounts kill your business. If you don't know what you stand for, you will go with the flow and the flow might not get you home. The flow might destroy your marriage because if you are not clear about what you stand for, people will convince you to give away your value proposition for less than what is worth and, in that way, no value will be created for yourself and the enterprise as a result, you will have limited resources to keep the house functional, and the strain from that might result in divorce.

Know when to say NO, especially when you are a small business that can't afford to give things for free or at huge discounts. Generally, I find that people are not comfortable paying a Black business the same rates/ fees they would pay a white or big business or a woman the same as a man. I have an idea why they do that, but it is a lot of factors, some are subjective, but some have been proven already in research; but I suspect in some cases, it's more about mind-set than anything else and some do it unconsciously.

Maybe also the legacy of apartheid has done more damage to our minds than we dare to accept and because we don't acknowledge that fact, the beliefs that were engraved in our minds sit in our subconscious and continue to control our behaviours more than we realise. We still see a white individual as superior to a Black person, similarly we see a man as superior to a woman, thus the inclination to pay the other more and as soon as we have to pay those we unconsciously see as inferior, we get into negotiation mode.

Freudian theory: The unconscious mind governs behaviour to a greater degree than people suspect. "Until you make the unconscious conscious, it will direct your life and you will call it fate" (C.G. Jung).

Because you can supply the same service or product as your competitor (i.e., big corporate) and they will be more comfortable paying higher to your competitor than to you, sometimes they just don't trust you will give them the same service but never trust even after you have delivered contrary to their beliefs. Unconscious bias, some call it.

Excel in what you do, don't put the Black business, BEE or SMME in disrepute. Your service determines if the customer will trust the next business that looks like you or not. Being black is not a value proposition, be so good that you can compete with your value proposition outside being black. You can't build a sustainable business by selling blackness or womanness. Gender and race can open certain doors for you because of our country's policies for sure but that won't keep you in business long enough or sustain you if you have nothing more to offer once the door opens.

Once an opportunity door opens, make sure you make a strong statement that won't be forgotten. A statement that says being black, woman, youth, small is not synonymous with bad quality, late delivery, half-done products, and bad customer service. Unfortunately, sometimes to make this point you have to do 10 times more than what your competitor has to do to get the same results.

Let's flip the coin a bit and talk to customers and potential customers

Customers, if you find yourself forever negotiating prices with a small business, but don't negotiate with a big business, you have a problem. This applies to youth, women and black, if you are always negotiating with these groupings but don't with their competitors, it is time to ask yourself questions. Why? If the value proposition is good, then pay for value and if it's not then don't. Don't squeeze blood out of the disadvantaged groups just because they are desperate to get that first client. Pay for value and if you can't afford it then have the courtesy to pass and go where you can afford the value you want.

Why do you have a problem paying someone who is giving you value for your money but just because s/he is small, black, youth then you want to pay less. Why always ask for pro bono work from someone just because they fall under the groups stated above. Be consistent and sometimes be more lenient even if you were going to ask for pro bono don't ask from SMME, black, young and woman businesses, it's hard enough for them. Don't make it even harder for them just because you know they need your order, so you take advantage of that. These are things most entrepreneurs won't be comfortable engaging their potential clients about, because they want the order so to have a conscience and pay for value.

Procurement officials, please stop asking SMMEs to pay you a facilitation fee, they don't have the resources to carry such expenses, otherwise, they will never grow because they have to take their profit and give it to you while you are getting your salary, don't be greedy if your salary is not enough, get a legitimate side hustle. I am not saying ask big businesses to pay you a facilitation fee but I am intentionally driving the idea that small businesses need to grow, and they need every penny to do that. Facilitation fees and unreasonable discounts are an enemy to SMME growth and sustainability.

We are building the country together and we need the economy to grow so next time you think of it know that you are killing your fellow citizen and that's not African, it's not Ubuntu. Selfishness is not an African thing, but a colonial thing where people believe in exclusivity. I must get for myself at the expense of the other who I don't believe has the right to breathe the same oxygen I breathe; she must get less quality oxygen just because she is different from me or just because I am greedy.

Business owners *"nani phela"* (You too in Zulu) deliver what you promised, don't play games", you can't afford to do that, you mess up for a lot more people than just yourself. Unfortunately, you have to be ten times better than your competitor to be deemed excellent or worth the same value. But push until even those who undermine black, youth, women and small business owners start slowly realising you are a force that they can't ignore; you are good at what you do, and epitomize excellence even if they would want to believe differently.

Let's talk about a few tools that can help you design a good value proposition and deliver it with amazing efficiency.

Tools to help you pave the way and understand your customer needs and operations better.

It's interesting how we always talk about Value Proposition but sometimes we don't even pay attention to whether the people we are designing the value proposition for, would like it. Value Propositions change every day because those who are to receive the value-add change every day too. Their problems and needs evolve and that means what is on offer has to change continuously to remain relevant.

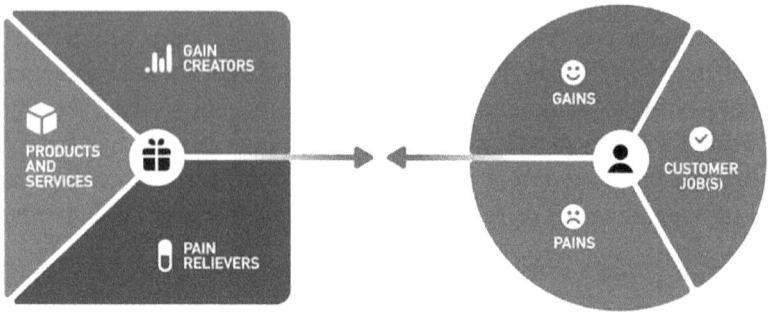

Figure 10: Value Proposition Canvas
Source: *Osterwalder & Pigneur (2010)*

Don't spend too much time building a product and a service based on your assumptions and feelings. Test the product as soon as possible. It's like spending lots and lots of time preparing a meal for your husband on the assumption that he likes dumpling and stew mixed with chakalaka. Only to find out after spending the money and time that your husband likes peanut butter and bread which was going to cost you less money and time, thus getting him more excited and happier for a longer time for your effort. You would have addressed the real need by taking care of the pain of craving peanut butter and bread.

The danger of assumptions and the losses that come with it are not worth it. Talk to your husband/potential client sooner rather than later and find out what he likes and what excites him. You have the power, skill, knowledge, and experience to make it better for him.

This method of going to market to find out early is called the lean startup principle which was developed by Eric Ries in a quest to help startups go to market lean without breaking the bank. Then Prof Steve Blank added to those principles what he called the customer discovery and development process where he gives you the step-by-step process of how you can get to know your customer leanly.

Additionally, Alexander Osterwalder and Yves Pigneur developed the tools to operationalise this and the tool to profile the customer is called the Value Proposition Canvas (VPC) which helps you capture the customer needs and the value you are promising in a more systematic and structured way. Once you understand the customer, what she needs and how she needs it, then you need to develop the product or service and figure out what you need to do on a day-to-day basis to deliver it the way it is needed. That takes us to another tool developed by Alexander Osterwalder and Yves Pigneur called the Business Model Canvas (BMC) which works well with design thinking processes.

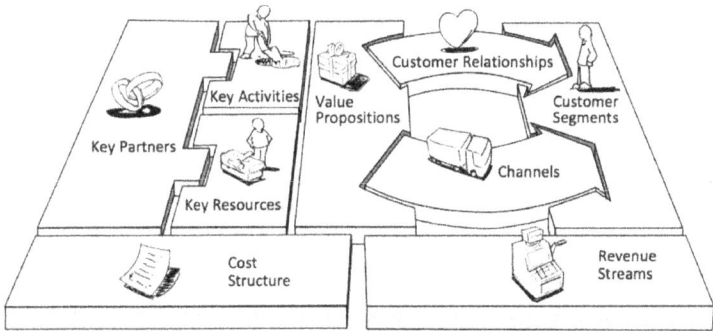

Figure 11: Business Model Canvas
Source: *Osterwalder & Pigneur (2010)*

You need to be very clear on what and to whom you will need to produce your value proposition for your product. Know where you will produce it and how you will get it to the client after producing it. Who will help you get it to the client? Answering all these might sound daunting if you don't have a tool to help you do this in a structured way. The business model canvas is that tool that can guide you through the process. Don't start with a thick pretty business plan, start with this simple tool to build a model.

If you need funding or if it is needed by external stakeholders, then you can develop the business plan. If you don't need it, don't do it, it takes a lot of time and by the time you are done with it so much has changed that you need to go back and alter it. I am not saying you shouldn't plan when I say, 'don't do the business plan', what I mean is that don't do it the traditional way, use these flexible tools. However, you have the flexibility to change the BMC as many times as possible since it does not require you to prettify it. It's an agile tool for people on the move during VUCA times.

If you want to read more about these (VPC and BMC) tools and the theories behind them, look for a book which is authored by Alexander Osterwalder and Yves Pigneur titled Business Model Generation: A handbook for visionaries, game changers and challengers. What is the book about? Business Model Generation (2010) is a comprehensive guide to building innovative business models. From empathising and connecting with customers to finding inspiration for products and learning from some of today's most game-changing platforms, these blinks will help you kick-start your business thinking.

LETTER

9

THE ENVIRONMENT, ENTERPRISE AND THE ENTREPRENEUR INTEGRATED (3-IN-1)

MrE, was the environment conducive enough for our marriage to work? Was it, or did I miss something? Was there anything that I needed to prepare before saying "I do"? Did I miss all the signs that suggested we were not going to last? Why didn't you hint? You have divorced many times, you must have seen the signs and the naivety on my side. You should have warned me. Perhaps I would have listened, maybe I would have prepared better, I would have gone for the pre-marital counselling and came prepared. But, would the pre-marital counselling have helped, was I going to grasp anything from there? I see the divorce rate is high from both sides, is there any empirical evidence that those who go for pre-marital counselling make it. Should I have dated you longer before marrying you? Was that going to change anything?

All these are questions that lingered on my mind since the day we divorced. I don't have the answers. I am hoping you will answer me MrE, please answer me. Maybe your answers will help others who are eyeing marrying you to prepare better.

Did I miss all the red flags, or did you miss all the red flags? Who missed what? And how do we make sure that those who come after me don't miss the red flags? Is it even a reasonable expectation to expect that in our human capacity we are capable of seeing the red flags and mitigating them up-front while enjoying the feeling of butterflies?

Yours In Love

MsE

My observation is that there are just too many moving objects to pay attention to and worry about, is it even possible to mitigate the risk that each of them brings to the table, because when you are married you don't only worry about yourself. You have to think about your hubby, house, your in-laws and all that comes with it. In the entrepreneurship world, when you marry MrE you have to think about self (The Entrepreneur), the home (The enterprise) and the Environment (The external factors) where your home is and most of these are out of your control. All these factors affect your marriage, and they can make or break it if you don't pay attention to them.

Figure 12 shows all the moving objects you have to be comfortable dealing with. It comes in 6 layers and all need MsE to manage and navigate.

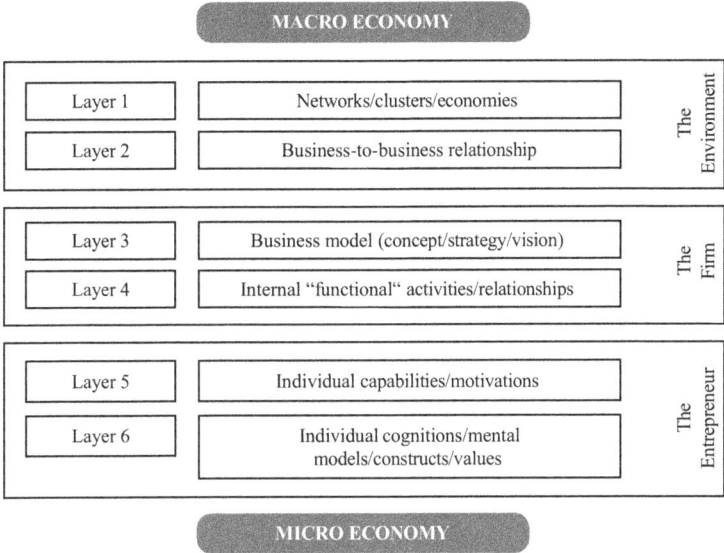

Figure 12: Ontological layers in the small firm domain
Source: *Fuller and Moran (2001, p. 54)*

The figure above summarises the number of things involved and the things that need to be managed to make the marriage work and all this needs to be managed by one person "the wife" MsE. 24/7 you need to know what is happening on each of the different levels of your business/marriage.

Self-care – "You can't pour from an empty cup, worse if you don't even have the cup". While managing all these factors, one needs to take care of self. It's a lot and one has to be able to manage it all. All these happen in an ecosystem, and the awareness of that ecosystem is key for the success of anyone and everyone.

Overview of the entrepreneurship ecosystem

I call this observing of everything an integrated approach to managing your marriage. The entrepreneurship ecosystem refers to the collective and systemic nature of entrepreneurship. It's a complex system best explained by complex theory. All the elements in the system are interconnected, interdependent and interrelated; that is why it is not easy to manage it because if one node/element in the system suffers, the replica effect is impactful as it affects all the other elements in the system. The Global Entrepreneurship Monitor (GEM) Framework recognises that entrepreneurship is part of a complex feedback system from inputs, through activity to outputs, and finally, outcomes and impacts. What GEM is highlighting here, is the nature of the complexity of the system where its inputs, outputs and impact interact. So, I am sharing here different diagrams to help you picture and appreciate what you need to manage as an entrepreneur for awareness of your risks and opportunities. It is difficult to manage what you don't know; be aware, familiarise yourself with all the moving objects and decide which ones are applicable to you and worth spending more time on monitoring. The tricky thing about external factors is that you can't change them, you need to change yourself and everything you have control over; based on what is happening externally that you don't have control over.

Within these three dimensions, the environment, which is the only part the entrepreneur has no control over, are its complexities that need to be managed. Daniel Isenberg used what he calls an entrepreneurship ecosystem to illustrate some of these domains.

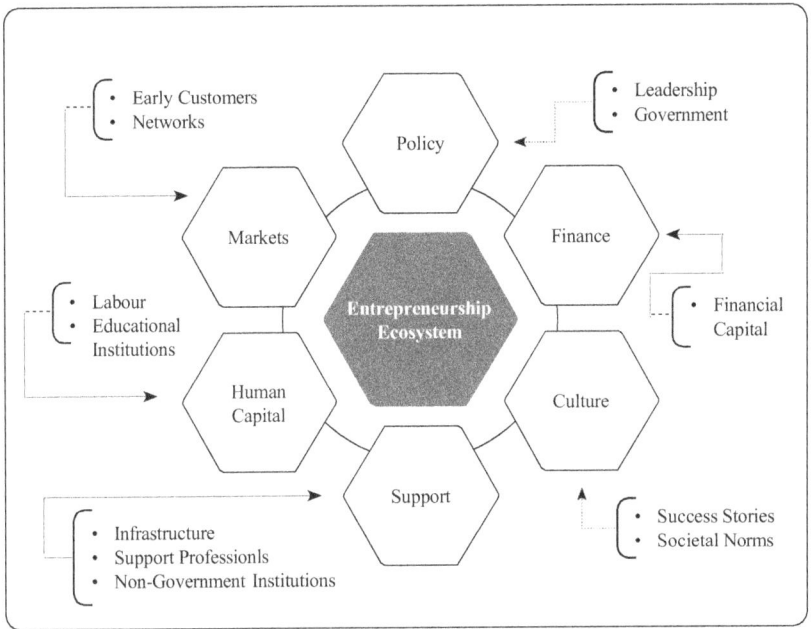

Figure 13: Entrepreneurship Ecosystem
Source: *Isenberg (2011)*

Lesson: Be ready to manage complexities, otherwise if you can't handle them then you won't make it in entrepreneurship, that or you're going to stay at a very micro level.

L E T T E R

HIGH DIVORCE RATE (± 90% FAIL)

Dear MrE

Why do you choose to enrich just a few, less than 10% and destroy the lives of over 90%, after they chose to love and be committed to you? The other burning question that has been persistent in my mind that I wished to ask you is 'why the high divorce rate'? According to research, it is said that as high as up to 90% of the marriages end up in divorce but strangely that has not stopped many from still getting married. What is the secret to staying married to you, MrE, what are the factors that cause this high divorce rate, some of the marriages don't even get to 3 years and very few make it beyond 3 years, why? Another interesting observation is that some who divorce you end up remarrying. They come back to you after they have spent most of their life married to MrEm, but they don't seem to get the perfect man and come back to you. It is evident that once someone has had a relationship with you, it becomes difficult to go back and continue as if one never met you. The question is, why can't a person divorce you and go marry "MrEm" and live happily ever after. What makes you so addictive that if someone marries you once, they can't live without you after divorce?

Yours in love

MsE

Let's talk about that a little, MrE, before we even have this conversation. We talk of divorce, failure and remarrying and someone listening to us having this conversation might wonder what exactly we are referring to so let's bring it home and define the terminologies we are using.

First, what is failure? What are we referring to when we talk of divorce and failure rates? The dictionary refers to failure as "the neglect or omission of expected or required action" or "the state or condition of not meeting a desirable or intended objective" It's important to note that this is a process, and not an event; it does not happen overnight, it's a slow process that if you don't pay attention to it, you might miss the signs and only see it at the end and think it was an event.

Failure is not a surprise, every business person ought to know when his/her business is about to fail. There are red flags when the process starts, it makes you uncomfortable and you start wondering.

Tip: Create a list of things/indicators to watch out for and those things should be the red flags one monitors so when you see them you know the failure process has started so you can be proactive. Have a list of green, amber, and red flags. Monitor these, they are your indicators of how your business is doing and be clear on what action you need to take when given a situation. Don't wait until it is too late to remedy the situation. The over-optimistic, unrealistic, and over-confident are the ones who will fail and eventually succeed. Those who don't see the stumbling blocks, the threats, their weaknesses, and the impossibilities.

But most of the time, the over-optimistic nature of entrepreneurs leads them not to act quickly enough because even when the red flags are there, they remain over-confident and optimistic that things will eventually work out. Thus, it is important to have a soundboard, coach, mentor, or someone you can bounce your thoughts off, so when you start to ignore real red flags then that person can be the one who says, 'watch out'. In addition to the red flag checklist you have for yourself that you monitor.

But you as an entrepreneur must still be alert and you can't take your eyes off the ball, you still need to keep your eyes and ears open in case your soundboard misses it. The idea is to have more than one pair of eyes to give comfort that someone will pick it up, it can't be everyone missing the red flags.

"Failure is the best thing that can ever happen to you as an entrepreneur, at same time, the most painful thing you will ever have to deal with in this journey". As painful and undesirable as it is, everyone needs a dose of it. The questions I always ask MrE, which I hope he will help me answer is. Why the 90% divorce rate/failure? Why is it so difficult for many entrepreneurs to have a lasting relationship with MrE? "The happily ever after, is it a myth?"

As much as I say to myself, I wish someone had told me how hard it was going to be and that I was most likely going to fail, I wonder if I were going to listen and how that would have changed my decision and actions.

I probably wasn't going to listen as I was crazily in love, I had already fallen for MrE, it was going to be difficult to stand up and walk away but still, I wish someone told me the whole story. Was it going to make me feel better failing knowing I was told or is it better failing saying it's because I did not know? After all, does it change anything whether I knew the full story, or I knew the end at the beginning? I doubt it and the general trend suggests people still marry MrE anyway, regardless. Once you have been with MrE, it is difficult to detach completely, most come back, and the figure below tries to illustrate the unending cycle linearly and simplistically once you have tasted being with MrE.

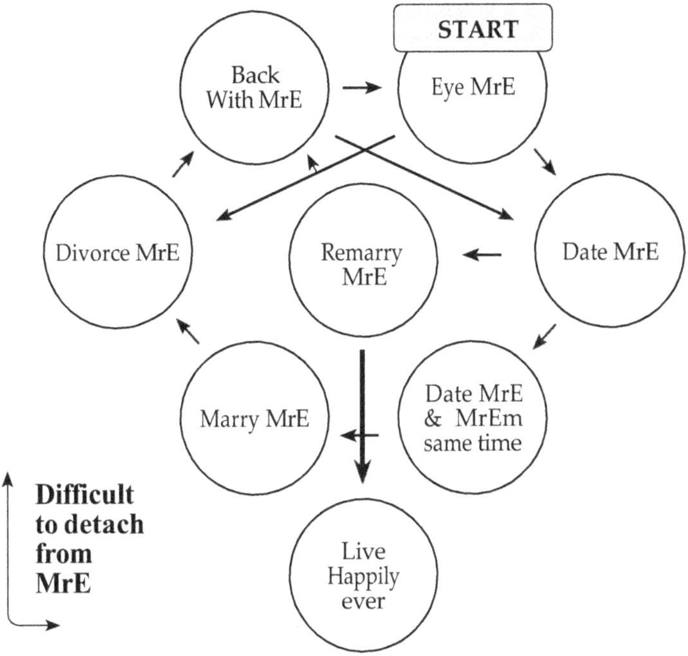

Figure 14: Unending cycle of divorcing and remarrying MrE
Source: *Author's own construction*

The same thing that causes you to fail multiple times is the very thing that will make you succeed eventually

It sounds contradictory, how can the very same thing that caused your failure cause your success too? Let's unpack it a little more so you understand better. How people think plays a big role in how they will act and behave. This is even deeper than what people think it is, also informed by what people believe of themselves and their values. Entrepreneurs think very highly of themselves, their capacity to do things, and their ability to control outcomes. They believe they can control the outcome, they believe it is within their powers to achieve certain things. They generally have an internal locus of control unlike some who believe their life is controlled somewhere by someone else which we call the external locus of control.

If we were to use the Freudian theory from which the iceberg model emanates, you will realise below the surface stuff of entrepreneurs (beliefs, values) which no one sees, is what leads them to lead there.

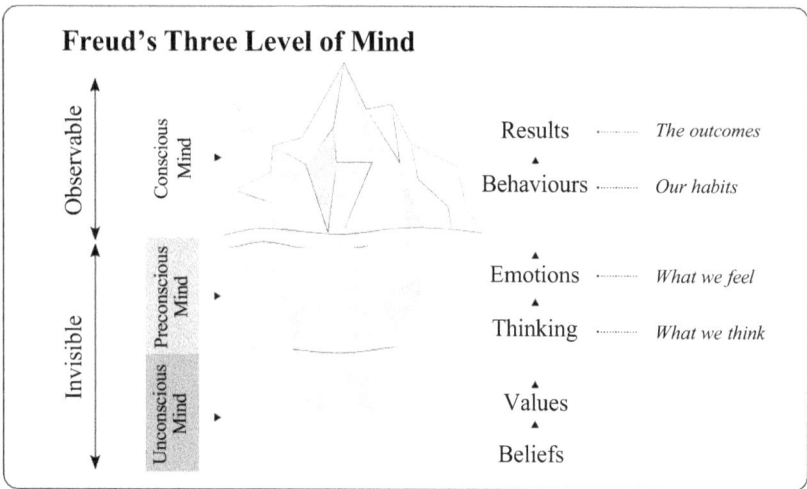

Figure 15: Freud's Iceberg theory model
Source: *Author's integration of Freud and Iceberg Models*

Below the iceberg sits a belief system that says I can do it, I have what it takes to do it and this is where the over-optimism comes into play. Entrepreneurs decision-making process (judgement and choices) is deeply rooted in the things I mentioned earlier, the over-optimistic, unrealistic and over-confident attitude. Think about over-optimistic or over-confident individuals and how they approach life in general.

Kahneman and Cools and Van den Broek find a way to explain how entrepreneurs think and act. He used the concept of cognitive styles. Cognitive style is defined as a preferred and habitual/consistent way that different individuals organise, represent, and perceive or process information and experiences. The understanding of the different cognitive styles should add value to understanding how entrepreneurs learn, solve problems, make decisions, become creative and even perceive risks and opportunities (Kahneman, 2011). The quality/attribute that makes entrepreneurs fail and eventually succeed is 'heuristic bias'; this is what most entrepreneurs suffer from : Over-optimistic, confident, perception of opportunity versus threats.

Is being over-optimistic and unrealistic a bad or good thing in entrepreneurship? Is it not true that the very reason that makes entrepreneurs fail several times is the very thing that makes them eventually succeed? It does not sound logical, but it is true. How can the very attribute that makes you fail, make you succeed? When you are over-optimistic and confident you attempt big things, and go for big opportunities. Because you over-estimate yourself you fail, but you never give up and you do this repeatedly and in that process, you become better because you learn, you grow, you gain skills and eventually in your 10th or 11th attempt you get it right. Since you have practised enough and you know better, you have developed skills you did not have before. Those who are not over-optimistic and over-confident, will not grow at the same pace as their counterpart, and they learn more slowly thus reducing their chances of getting it right eventually. And if you look at what I just explained above, you will notice that it fits system 1 perfectly as shown in Table 3.

Kahneman tried to categorise entrepreneurs' thinking into two, as shown in the table below. He termed the two categories system 1 which is automatic; system 2 which is effortful and entrepreneurs prefer the automatic system and in Cools terminologies, this falls under the intuitive and creative cognitive style.

Table 3: Kahneman's Systems of Thinking

System 1 (Automatic)	System 2 (Effortful)
Intuitive	Analytical
Fast thinking	Slow thinking
Spontaneous	Deliberate
Heuristics/systematic error	Reasoning
Impulsive and emotional	Self-control
Experiencing self	Remembering self

Source: *Kahneman (2011) as cited in Galawe (2017)*

Let's unpack it, if you are over-optimistic, unrealistic, and over-confident, always over-estimating yourself; you will go for every opportunity that is presented to you, even if you don't have what it takes to successfully execute it. Because you over-estimated yourself and are confident that you can execute, only to find out you can't, you will attempt all these opportunities and fail. But every time you attempt and fail, you learn; your knowledge, skills and experience improve. Then by the time you overestimate yourself for the 1000th time, you know better how to execute, still very optimistic that you will achieve what you set out to achieve.

Only over-optimistic people try hard things, they assess situations and see opportunities rather than see risks and threats and because of that, they will throw themselves in there and guess what - they learn, grow and eventually, their expert intuition becomes stronger and they can assess situations quicker and analyse them correctly.

For example, if a decision needs to be made quickly by an expert, he can use his intuition to make a more accurate decision, and this is referred to as expert intuition[15]. This is where entrepreneurs come in as experts in the "trial and error fail method" and everything becomes clearer, and their intuition is more awake and they start winning.

The findings from my PhD show that entrepreneurs who use a lot of intuition, who are creative and innovative, who are motivated by on-going innovation and always push boundaries, run successful businesses. It was also evident from the same study that more entrepreneurs (>80%) prefer intuitive rather than analytic styles when making decisions. The concept of cognitive styles comes from Kahnemen's book "Think fast and slow" where he talks about three styles (planning, analytical and intuitive/creative).

He says intuitive or creative styles are used by default as they don't require a lot of effort and time as compared to the planning and analytical cognitive styles. He calls these "system 1 and system 2" as shown in Table 3. What's the difference between those who eventually succeed versus those who end up giving up?

(Murmann & Sardana, 2013)[15]

Those who succeed, do they succeed while still being unrealistic and over-optimistic? Yes, they keep on being unrealistic, and over-optimistic and finally they get it right. Those who don't succeed are either realistic or lose their optimistic approach as a result of the multiple failures.

I believe that the entrepreneur needs to have or use a certain degree of each of the two cognitive styles depending on what phase the business is in. You can't only rely on intuition because the sweet spot is found in analytical, planning and intuition, then I believe instead of failing 100 times before making it, you might just fail 50 times and get to your Canaan earlier .

(Disclaimer – these numbers are hypothetical and are not meant to suggest that you will succeed at trial 50 or 100. They are only used to illustrate a concept)

Tip: Balance the planning, analysis, and intuition and that will give you the secret to your success. As you get more experienced, and your intuition becomes stronger and more accurate; you increase the planning and analysis but still find the sweet spot, according to your experience and failures. Remember, earlier I spoke about the green, amber and red lights which you can use to monitor how you are doing, let's look at some of the 20 things you can monitor or pay attention to mitigate.

The 20 signs or symptoms of a failing small business

How do you know your business is about to fail?

There are always red flags, and they don't just show up one day as red flags, it is a very slow long process and if you are woke, you will notice when it starts moving from Green to Orange and eventually to Red. When loans start substituting your income, for example, you always run to loans to pay for overheads and process orders. Look out for the signs below and do something about them, be more proactive, rather than wait until it's too late to do something.

Red flag 1.   When all your suppliers start closing your credit lines because you can't keep your promises anymore, you're either late or can't pay.

Red flag 2.   When the bank cancels your overdraft and credit lines.

Red flag 3.   When you have no money to process orders and you don't even have the means to get credit to do this anymore.

Red flag 4.   When you keep selling at a loss with the hope of future profitable orders. Accepting orders at a loss is a no, no.

Red flag 5.   When your only competitive advantage is price while your clients are looking for more than price. No value proposition to offer clients.

Red flag 6.   When you keep on doing the same things you did the previous year when you made a loss.

Red flag 7.   No profit and cash flow for an extended period (Big corporates can afford to manage such but not an SMME).

Red flag 8.   Negative cash flow that hinders you from actioning anything.

Red flag 9.   When your expenses are increasing faster than your income for a prolonged period.

Red flag 10. Growing at the wrong time without understanding the economic outlook and the potential impact.

Red flag 11. Trying to pay big corporate salaries to motivate salespeople to perform instead of paying less and rewarding those who perform with extra money. When this yields you the opposite result but you are not stopping.

Red flag 12. When you don't know how deep your pockets are and how long they can sustain you.

Red flag 13. Not monitoring staff and putting pressure on delivery and penalising those who do not meet the target.

Red flag 14. Having no stringent quality control measures and ensuring that customers sign off "samples" before final production.

Red flag 15. Taking too long to act (i.e. not cutting costs quick enough to minimise the risk of failure during recession/ pandemic, cut your losses while you can).

Red flag 16. Taking wrong advice from people who never ran their own businesses. Listen, assess and make your own decision, advice is advice it is not meant to be taken raw or even taken for that matter if it does not make sense.

Red flag 17. Leaving 100% of your business in other people's hands, people who do not have the same or better skills and interests as you.

Red flag 18. Being blind to Industry dynamics versus shifts in the country.

Red flag 19. Having only one client for a prolonged period without getting any new clients.

Red flag 20. Customer numbers dwindling.

When did my business start failing?

Just a short story; my business started failing while I was busy getting awards and winning competitions, when everyone was praising me for doing well; the process of failure was unfolding behind the scenes. Don't let people's praises, winning competitions, being on TV and radio or being a speaker everywhere fool you. That is good, but it does not necessarily mean you are successful, the devil is in the detail that no one else sees but you. Don't let those things make you take your eyes off what matters.

When I won SAB kickstart regional awards and was nominated for the national, my business was already bleeding but when I entered the competition, I was still fine as all the financials I submitted were still showing growth, profits and a good forecast, no one knew things were about to change for the worst. The winnings were based on past performance but what was happening at the time when I was receiving the awards was a different story. The process had started, and it was moving very fast on a downward trajectory.

I remember I was invited to SAFM Nancy's woman show. The presenter congratulated me and told me "the sky is the limit", she sees a very bright future for me as a Black woman. After that interview, a lot of people who knew me, and listened to the interview called and congratulated me on the awards, but I was bleeding inside because things were not looking as glossy on the inside as they were on the outside. My marriage with MrE was in tatters, we looked like the perfect couple, but behind the scenes we were not happy at all. The recession had started, and I was losing contracts and clients fast. Governments had changed in the Western Cape and supplying schools directly with learning material was becoming a challenge as the procurement policy of schools changed and section 20 schools had to procure via the dept. of education. When it came to textbooks, they had to buy directly from publishers cutting us small businesses out of the equation. Even for the section 21 schools, things changed in the learning material procurement process.

My business had about three (school stationery and learning material, corporate stationery and promotional items) revenue streams focusing on schools and corporates. I supplied schools with textbooks, stationery, uniforms, and cleaning material so when government changed, the revenue stream from schools suffered as the rules of the game changed. The second revenue stream mainly focused on corporates, I supplied The second with office stationery and when the recession hit, they started to be very careful on how they spent their money so price became a big thing and most of them moved to bigger stationery suppliers as they could supply them at a cheaper price. The third revenue stream was also from corporates supplying corporate clothing and gifts so when the recession hit, this one suffered too as corporates started to spend their money on essential items and corporate gifts and clothing were a luxury item so that went downhill as well. Subsequently, the contracts I had for this revenue stream were not renewed, and even those that were still active, the budget for them decreased drastically.

I had a mentor who was assigned to me, Mr Wajdi Abrahams, who kept saying "you need to tighten the belt sister things are going to get worse". He could not make decisions on my behalf, he could only make me aware, but the over-optimistic me, did not think it was that bad. I thought it would get better soon and I kept my overheads as they were (staff and offices). Little did I know that he was right, he was reading the economic trends and outlook reports correctly. It got tighter and tighter, and I was squeezed more and more every day until I could not breathe.

I remember in 2010/11, I was nominated for the Western Cape Business Opportunities Forum (WECBOF) business award. I first accepted the nomination but later on withdrew, because as much as what I was nominated for was true and it was an achievement, I knew that by the time I received the award or soon just after that, my business would be visibly dying. I withdrew for integrity's sake, and this talks to the fact that failure is a process and the fact that you were doing well two years ago does not guarantee that you will be doing well three years to come. Therefore, you must always be thinking of how best to make your business better, more resilient, and competitive. It is a very uncertain world, they call it a VUCA world, and things change all the time, and they change fast. You can be successful today and lose it all tomorrow. So, stay humble and be open to learning every day.

I did well when it was my time to do well and I was nominated and won a few competitions: SAB kickstart regional award, SAB kickstart national nominee, Technoserve business plan competition and WECBOF business of the year competition. These were all the things that confirmed to me I was on the right track, I was doing something right, but business is business; nothing is guaranteed for life and small mistakes sometimes compound and reverse all the other good work you have done. "Don't let awards and media attention fool you, it's not necessarily a sign of success." I am grateful for my failure, otherwise I wouldn't have a PhD in entrepreneurship, and I would not be authoring this book. It was worth it, the pain, frustrations and the failures were the school fees I had to pay for my entrepreneurship education. Live learning NQF level 11 if ever there was such. It was all worth it.

Why didn't my business plan shield my business from failure?

My business plan could not help me see the signs because it was not written by me, and it was not a document I used to operate my business. It was a pretty document meant to impress funders when I was looking for funding. Umsobomvu paid a consultant for me to have such a pretty business plan. The business plan said all things are good, I will be making profits and profits and profits. Not to discredit the consultant who helped me with the business plan, but it was unrealistic, and he did it based on the unrealistic information I gave him. First, the margins were off because I did not understand the industry so I thought I had luxury on the mark-ups I could put on my products, but I was so wrong.

The margins, especially for the stationery, were very thin as the industry was saturated and the competition was tough. When I started selling, I was trading far lower than what was in the business plan. At least, for the corporate clothing and gifts, the margins were flexible there. Additionally, textbooks also had a fixed margin which the publishers gave you so they had a retail and wholesale price and everyone had to sell using the same retail price otherwise you would be more expensive than the competition. Anyway schools had the price lists themselves already, so you had to sell at that price. The good thing was during the SAB kickstart training and the Technoserve business planning competition, we had to rework our business plans with more understanding and that's where I got to realise how unrealistic my mark-ups were and how difficult it was going to be to compete with such prices as the competition was selling lower.

Here are a few lessons I learned in the process:

Lesson 1: First do your research and have a basic understanding of the industry dynamics.

Lesson 2: Do your own business plan to understand the basics and what will make your business work or not work. You can give the consultant to beautify it, but understand the core that makes it.

Lesson 3: Listen to your mentors and do something about the warnings they give you.

Lesson 4: Don't ignore external factors and economic trends.

Lesson 5: Act fast to either increase your revenue or cut overheads to at least stay on a breakeven point.

Lesson 6: Even if you are over-optimistic that things won't go south still make provision for if they do go as bad as you have been warned.

Lesson 7: Give yourself credit for attempting big things even when they don't work out, it takes courage to take on big opportunities.

Why didn't the loans sustain me financially?

Loans can only take you so far and at some point, you need to generate money from sales otherwise you won't be able to pay back the loans. If you have no turnaround strategy don't keep taking loans because you're going to fail with big debt. Loans are meant to help you and not to be the source of income or revenue. When loans start substituting income or sales then you know it's time to pivot, review your business model or do something to change the situation. This will sound contrary to popular belief but sometimes it is best to give up; "what do I mean about that?" give up on trying to save the business if you don't see the light at the end of the tunnel and invest your energies in something new where you see light at the end.

Over-optimism can sometimes keep you barking for too long at a dead horse while you can cut your losses and go start something new that has potential. These are never easy decisions to make because most of the time you wonder "what if I give up when I'm just about to get my breakthrough". That's where the balance of analysis, planning and intuition needs to come in to make those serious decisions. I don't regret giving up in 2011 and closing my first business, it sounds bad to say you gave up but sometimes you also need a break especially when you get so tired that your creative juices don't even flow anymore, you are just surviving and hanging along.

It is ok to take a break, you need to give yourself that permission when it is time to do so then you can come back stronger and better which is what I did and I am wiser today than when I started the first business.

Something to nibble on

Giving up is not always bad, context matters. The trick is knowing, when the right time to give up is. The right time to give up was when I relocated to Johannesburg, went back to corporate and started a new life altogether. My question to you: Is there something you need to let go of? Give up on it so you can look at new opportunities. The negative side is that if you hold on to something that is not working for too long you deprive yourself of the opportunity to start something new.

Sometimes it is ok to give yourself permission to take a break, take it slow and do something else. I did, I was off entrepreneurship for 3 years before going back. During that time I became an employee, tried to recover financially and get my confidence back. Moreover, get my creative juices flowing again. I also had the time to reflect and decide what kind of business was suitable for me and exactly what I am passionate about. The mistakes I made in the past I don't want to repeat but, thankfully, it worked out for the best in the end. Interestingly, during this time I discovered that my passion is people development this is when I moved to teaching, mentorship and coaching.

Why my mentors couldn't help me either

A mentor is there to support you, guide you and share her experiences with you but she will never run the business for you. Also, it is up to you how you make the best of their skills and experience. They take no responsibility for your failure or success. You make it happen or not happen. Trust me, mentors are important to have particularly entrepreneurs because you can easily get caught up in your perfect unrealistic world sometimes, that you miss certain things that an experienced mentor will pick up and warn you about.

Listening is very important when you have a mentor, hear them first, apply your mind, then action. Don't take too long, the business world only has a fast lane, no driving on the left, otherwise you will die a slow death.

LETTER

11

A SPECIAL LETTER TO ALL WOMEN WHO ARE ASPIRING AND ACHIEVING

Dear women entrepreneurs, executives, leaders and professionals

Let's have the conversation, woman to woman

Let me start by saying we were all born to be **GREAT**, we have so much **GREATNESS** within us, and our gender, age or race will never change that. We are the only people who can change that, if we believe we are not **GREAT** because of our gender. Our belief is what we are going to demonstrate with our behaviour, if we think we are **GREAT** and have **GREATNESS** within us, that is exactly what is going to show up in our daily lives. Let's chat about a few things that hinder us from living our best lives and enjoying our **GREATNESS**. Firstly, it is the unbelief that operationalises itself and robs us of the **GREAT** life we deserve.

I won't trivialise the fact that some of us have really good reasons not to be **GREAT**, the environment around us preaches to us every day this message that because we are women or black, therefore we are not so **GREAT** or we don't have what it takes to be **GREAT**. This is a narrative we have the power to change regardless of the voices we hear. We are **GREAT**, we are born **GREAT**, we deserve to be **GREAT**, and we need to strive to be **GREAT**.

But what are the things that make us feel inadequate and how can we navigate around them or deal with them? In my experience as a coach, mentor, supervisor and senior lecturer, I have observed women very closely with a sore heart. This sore heart is caused by seeing how much potential and **GREATNESS** is out there, but people still live average lives because they are not aware or they are scared or just don't believe that, as women, they deserve to occupy spaces with authority and confidence. We grew up in communities where the women we saw every day did not plant a seed in us that we can be **GREAT** and we can do whatever we want. Let me affirm this to you, nothing has to delay us in taking up big opportunities and pushing ourselves to reach **GREATNESS**.

Depending on which generation you come from, if you are from the older generation, you probably grew up seeing women who were suppressed by a patriarchal and apartheid system that you thought what you saw was what **GREAT** is. You were never exposed to spaces where women are **GREATER** than what you have seen in your immediate surroundings. Thus, your **GREATNESS** was tainted and limited not even by the sky but the patriarchy and apartheid system that kept '**GREAT**' lower than the roof at your house. By the time you were exposed to **GREATER** than what you knew within that distorted, lowered ceiling then your belief system was already formed and strongly ingrained in you that it became a hassle to believe anything different.

We are **GREAT**, we are born to be **GREAT**, **GREATER** than what the systems that form our opinions can ever dictate but the question is, do you want to be **GREAT**, do you believe that you are **GREAT**, do you believe **GREATNESS** is for no one else but you. If you believe that but, you are scared, don't have confidence, and don't know how then, what do you do?

Here are a few tips as you Venture into your GREATNESS

It all starts with your belief system; what do you believe? If you believe contrary to what you suppose to, how do you then move forward and change your limiting belief?

1. The question is; how do you change a limiting belief?

2. Expose yourself to things and people **GREATER** than you have ever imagined, try to feel them and spend time around them.

3. Find a mentor who is living a life ideal to the one you want, learn from them, how did they move from where they were to where they are. Ask them to challenge your belief system and the way you do things and everything that limits you.

4. Get an accountability buddy, someone as ambitious as you but not jealous. Someone who gets excited by seeing you succeed and go for **GREATER** things than you have ever attempted. Hold each other accountable.

5. Have a Vision Board that scares you, one that you know when others see it, they will laugh at you and think you have gone crazy.

6. Then put a developmental plan together, how are you going to achieve what you have on your vision board and what resources do you need. Break it down into manageable small chunks.

7. Get a coach to help you stay on track and help you with your blind spots as you attempt to action your plans and achieve your yearly, monthly, quarterly, weekly and daily goals.

8. If there are things that are difficult to deal with from the past that are holding you back, get professional help, get a therapist, counsellor, psychologist, pastor, whomever you feel you need to help you talk it out and heal.

9. Start believing in yourself, your subconscious will stare at your belief, and your actions will slowly start following. Of course, you will have your mentor and/or coach to help you through the process.

10. Don't do it solo, we all need each other to succeed, have a support system and people who you know are with you and behind you.

11. Build internal strength and just keep pushing so that when your support doesn't support you at a certain time, you can draw from within.

12. Above all, believe in someone or something bigger than you as you are not 100% in control of everything. I am a Christian, so I believe in God and I trust Him to keep this machine (ME) operating and optimally functional.

13. Do your part as well; protect your mind, heart, and soul from anything that might not serve you.

14. Don't be scared to promote yourself, be comfortable talking about your strengths, what you do well and the value you bring to the table. No one else can do it better than you.

15. Don't be lazy, educate and up skill yourself always, be competent and be a woman of excellence. Make other younger women believe that **GREATNESS** is possible and achievable.

16. Inspire and uplift as you go up, don't carry the badge of being the first and only black or woman to achieve 1 2 3 too long. After some time, you must be proud that you are not the only woman anymore to achieve something because you brought someone with you as you went higher. Be uncomfortable if you are the only woman forever and no one after you.

17. As you venture into **GREATNESS**, the journey will ask you for sacrifices and one of them is TIME. The time you have has to be shared between social, health, business, career and family life. Whatever you want to make **GREAT** requires more than the average time you will spend on average things.

18. That brings me to my next point, the never ending guilt. Whatever you are busy with at any given time that brings a feeling of guilt and makes you feel like you are neglecting other things. It does not matter how much time you spend on each, you will always feel guilty about the time you are not spending on the other, and this is common with women. It is because subconsciously we think we can quantitatively balance or spend an equal amount of time on each area of our lives and still win or be **GREAT**.

I hate to break it to you but it's just not possible, especially when you are still building and you don't have the money to pay others to relieve you from other responsibilities. The likelihood is that your family and social life will suffer the most, manage that with care.

19. So how do you deal with the guilt? You have a conversation with yourself and decide what is acceptable and what is not acceptable, then qualitatively assign times for each part of your life and that is what should guide you as to whether you are doing well or not. Then have a conversation with those affected and explain that for such and such a period this is how you will spend your time and agree as to how you will use the little time you have as it won't be quantity, but quality, so you have to make the best of it. Does this mean you will wake up one day all guilt-free? No, it takes a long time to change a belief system that suggests that your success and being a good mom or wife is to sit at home, cook and be 100% quantitatively available for your family. If you decide to be that, it is **GREAT**, but if you decide to define success differently from the old norms then you have to be willing to deal with the internal conflicts. Trust me, there will be people as well who remind you of the old norms and want to tell you how much time you should quantitatively spend where. Remember you have a dream and you know how you want to do it and how you will make up for the quantity part of your lives. Big dreams can drown you so don't neglect what matters most chasing dreams endlessly.

20. Avoid trying to please everyone, you will fail dismally, especially when you get to a level of leadership that requires someone who can be straight and frank about issues. Know how to put your foot down as a woman but remain a woman. Have boundaries and know your boundaries are yours to manage so no one takes advantage of you just because you are a woman.

*Venture into **GREATNESS**!!!*
*"You were born to be **GREAT** so don't settle until you are **GREAT**"*

LETTER

12

A CHALLENGE TO ALL
ENTREPRENEURS

Take the challenge and write a letter to "Mr Entrepreneurship"

Dear entrepreneurs and aspiring entrepreneurs

This is an invite to you to keep the conversation going and learn from each other. To keep the conversation going, here is a challenge for you, once you are done reading the book, write a letter, just one letter. It is up to you whether you ask a question in that letter, tell "Mr Entrepreneurship" a story, vent your frustrations, or just appreciate what he has done for you or how he has changed your life.

Here is the brief: Imagine that entrepreneurship (the concept, activity and process) was a person. If you had an opportunity to write "Mr Entrepreneurship" a letter or have a conversation with him, what would you say or write in that letter? Write and share on any of our social media platforms @DrJBiz (Facebook, Twitter, Instagram, and LinkedIn). Feel free to either use text or graphics that best present what you want to say to him. Let's see how many letters we can get and what exciting stories will emerge from these letters. If we get enough good letters we will compile an eBook and share it for everyone's benefit.

Looking for 100 letters. Join the conversation @DrJBiz

Kind Regards ☺

DrJ

POEM!!

Whatever is shared in this book is a one-dimensional story of a complex multidimensional reality. A reality that can never be captured on a piece of paper by a pen, it's a story that no vocabulary is enough to articulate. It is a story that goes deeper than what the 23 alphabets can capture, a story that no human can tell with 100% accuracy as the human cannot comprehend and articulate the multidimensional complex reality of entrepreneurship. It's a story we try to understand and we will always be trying to understand until our systems shut down and we can't absorb or imagine any more. Even Artificial Intelligence (AI) cannot capture this story with 100% accuracy. It is a story that most think they understand and they can articulate but because of the complexity of this story even those who think they do, don't understand it because they don't have the capacity to understand that they don't understand, that it is more complex than what the brain can read into it. It is a story of an entrepreneur and the entrepreneurship process.

By DrJ

P A R T

DrJ SHORT BIO

Jabulile Msimango-Galawe (AKA DrJ) was born in a small village known as Mahushu in Mpumalanga – Nelspruit – Hazyview next to Kruger National Park Numbi Gate. She is a second-born with 8 siblings (3 brothers and 5 sisters). She did her primary school at Lundanda, higher primary at Mthimba and high school at Bhekiswako secondary school. She matriculated in 1994 with a dream of becoming a medical doctor but ended up spending one year at home teaching night school due to delayed matric results in Mpumalanga for certain schools for some subjects. The year she spent at home didn't turn out to be a waste, as she managed to get her driver's license and a bit of teaching experience.

She did her undergrad Degree BSc majoring in Statistics and Genetics at the University of the Free State in Bloemfontein, which she completed in 1999. She went on to do an MSc in Mathematical Statistics – Risk Analysis at the same university and graduated in 2002.

In 2013 she registered for her PhD in Entrepreneurship at Wits Business School and graduated in 2017. She also has a Certificate in Effective Mentoring and Coaching from the same Business School, which she acquired in 2020. DrJ is currently (2022) registered for a Master's by research as she is always looking at how she can enhance her knowledge and skill and this time by focusing her research on black leadership especially women and the role of coaching in developing black female leaders.

DrJ is a doctor of philosophy (entrepreneurship) and not a medical doctor, though she had a dream of becoming a medical Dr when she was young. You might ask what happened to the dream of becoming a medical doctor, did she give up on it? Here is an important story DrJ enjoys sharing about how she ended up being a statistician, with a PhD in entrepreneurship and not a medical doctor.

After completing matric, DrJ applied to study medicine but because her results were not good she ended up being accepted into BSc (Biological Sciences). The plan was to study BSc first year, pass with distinctions then move to medicine in the second year after passing the first year well. That's what DrJ was advised to do if she still wanted to be a medical doctor, unfortunately, she did not do well in her first year, she failed 50% of her courses and even those that she passed, she got exactly 50%. Consequently, she still didn't qualify to move to medicine.

She was in a hurry to complete her studies, get married and earn a salary. Option B was to complete her BSc which was going to take 4 years as she already added an extra year and only after that start medicine the second year which will take 6 years. She decided not to go into the medicine stream because it was going to take longer to complete, so she stayed with the BSc, and majored in Statistics and Genetics.

It was not in her career plans and vision as when she left home, she thought she was going to come back with a white coat, but she didn't. Looking back it was good. "I don't think I would have enjoyed the *injection job* and looking at ill people every day." Said DrJ

So that's how she let go of the dream of being a medical doctor to a PhD. She ended up doing statistics, the decision for her to do statistics was as a result of her getting distinctions, and it had nothing to do with what she wanted to do. She got distinctions in statistics and ended up getting a bursary to do MSc in statistics. That is how she became a statistician.

Fortunately, statisticians are in demand. She is never short of jobs or short on what to do. That was not in her plans but it worked out fine, *she says as she connects the dots backwards.* Though all these were not planned, she had no idea what a career plan was, how she needed to choose careers, why she should choose certain careers or what factors to consider. She just got lucky that it all came together and she enjoys doing the statistics jobs she ended up with though not intentionally chosen.

In a nutshell, she decided to enrol for a PhD specifically in entrepreneurship as a result of the failure of her first business. After her first business failed she promised herself that she was going to learn more about entrepreneurship so she can understand why up to 90% of the entrepreneurs who start businesses don't make it past 10 years of operation. She was part of these stats as well so she wanted to know why she failed and to find an equation that would help other entrepreneurs in the future to mitigate failure and understand what 1 + 1 equals to in entrepreneurship as it doesn't seem to add up to 2. So the PhD was therapeutic for her as it was a way to heal her deep scars resulting from the failure of her first business.

Something to nibble on

To the youth/younger generation, not everyone gets lucky, so start thinking about what you want to do and what you think you will enjoy. The worst thing is to find out after you have completed your undergrad or even postgrad that the career path you took does not suit you or the subjects you chose take you to a path you wouldn't have chosen if you knew. So spend time exploring what your passion is and combining that with what you are good at so you can be happier at work or running the type of business you choose.

They say sometimes in life, you can plan and things don't go the way you want so you become sad but sometimes when you look back and start connecting the dots, you see that there was a power higher than you that kind of like directed your steps that led you to be where you are today. That doesn't give you a license not to do your homework. Do your homework, research the careers and businesses you are interested in and then make decisions while allowing the man above to direct your path.

REFERENCES

1. Baum, J. R., & Locke, E. A. (2004). The relationship of entrepreneurial traits, skill, and motivation to subsequent venture growth. *Journal of Applied Psychology*, 89(4), 587.

2. Baum, J. R., Locke, E. A., & Smith, K. G. (2001). A multidimensional model of venture growth. *Academy of Management Journal*, 44(2), 292-303.

3. Blank, S. (2013a). *The four steps to the epiphany: successful strategies for products that win*: BookBaby.

4. Blank, S. (2013b). Why the lean startup changes everything? *Harvard business review*, 91(5), 63-72.

5. Busenitz, L. W., & Barney, J. B. (1997). Differences between entrepreneurs and managers in large organizations: Biases and heuristics in strategic decision-making. *Journal of Business Venturing*, 12(1), 9-30.

6. Chen, C. C., Greene, P. G., & Crick, A. (1998). Does entrepreneurial self-efficacy distinguish entrepreneurs from managers? *Journal of business venturing*, 13(4), 295-316.

7. Cools, E., & Van den Broeck, H. (2007). Development and validation of the Cognitive Style Indicator. *The Journal of psychology*, 14(1), 359-387.

8. Galawe, N. J. (2017). *Endogenous and exogenous risk factors in the success of South African small medium enterprises.* University of the Witwatersrand, Faculty of Commerce, Law and Management. Johannesburg

9. Isenberg, D. (2011). *The entrepreneurship ecosystem strategy as a new paradigm for economic policy: Principles for cultivating entrepreneurship.* Institute of International European Affairs, Dublin, Ireland.

10. Kahneman, D. (2011). *Thinking, fast and slow.* Macmillan.

11. Kirzner, I. M. (1978). Entrepreneurship, Entitlement, and Economic Justice. *Eastern Economic Journal,* 4(1), 9-25.

12. Kirzner, I. M. (1999). Creativity and/or Alertness: A Reconsideration of the Schumpeterian Entrepreneur. *Review of Austrian Economics,* 11(1), 5-17.

13. Knight. (1921). *Risk, uncertainty and profit.* New York: Cosimo Classics

14. Long, W. (1983). The meaning of entrepreneurship. *American Journal of small business*, 8(2), 47-59.

15. Mokgwatsane, L. Z. (2019). *Private Equity: Catalyst for Agricultural Entrepreneurship in South Africa.* Wits Business School, Faculty of Commerce, Law and Management, Johannesburg.

16. Murmann, J. P., & Sardana, D. (2013). Successful entrepreneurs minimize risk. *Australian Journal of Management,* 38(1), 191-215.

17. Osterwalder, A., & Pigneur, Y. (2010). *Business model generation: a handbook for visionaries, game changers, and challengers* (Vol. 1): John Wiley & Sons.

18. Reynolds, P. D., Hay, M., & Camp, S. M. (1999). *Global entrepreneurship monitor: 1999 executive report.* 3.

19. Ries, E. (2009). *Minimum viable product: a guide. Startup Lessons Learned.*

20. Ripsas, S. (1998). Towards an interdisciplinary theory of entrepreneurship. *Small Business Economics,* 10(2), 103-115.

21. Schumpeter, J. A. (1934). *The theory of economic development: An inquiry into profits, capital, credit, interest, and the business cycle.* 55.

22. Schumpeter, J. A. (2000). Entrepreneurship as innovation. *Entrepreneurship: The social science view,* 51-75.

23. Shane, S., & Venkataraman, S. (2000). The Promise of Entrepreneurship as a Field of Research. *Academy of Management Review,* 25(1), 217-226.

24. Vecchio, R. P. (2003). Entrepreneurship and leadership: common trends and common threads. *Human Resource Management Review,* 13(2), 303-327.

25. Venter, R., Urban, B., Beder, L., Oosthuizen, C., Reddy, C., & Venter, E. (2015). *Entrepreneurship: theory in practice:* Oxford University Press Southern Africa.

ISBN: 978-0-620-80009-9

www.ingramcontent.com/pod-product-compliance
Lightning Source LLC
Chambersburg PA
CBHW061158240326
R18026600001B/R180266PG41519CBX00029B/1